W9-CRG-421

The
Classic Book
of
Baby Names

1817

HARPER & ROW, PUBLISHERS, New York
Cambridge, Philadelphia, San Francisco, Washington
London, Mexico City, São Paulo, Singapore, Sydney

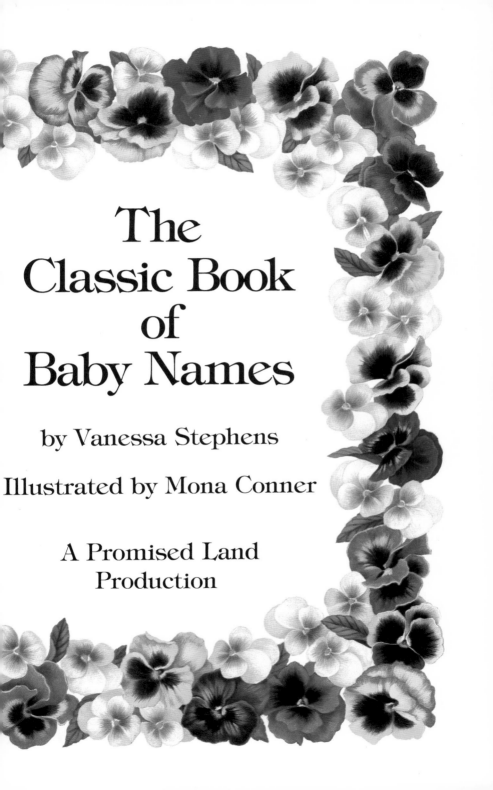

The
Classic Book
of
Baby Names

by Vanessa Stephens

Illustrated by Mona Conner

A Promised Land
Production

THE CLASSIC BOOK OF BABY NAMES. Text copyright © 1988 by Promised Land Productions, Inc. Illustrations copyright © 1988 by Mona Conner. All rights reserved. Printed in the United States of America. No part of this book may be used or reproduced in any manner whatsoever without written permission except in the case of brief quotations embodied in critical articles and reviews. For information address Harper & Row, Publishers, Inc., 10 East 53rd Street, New York, N.Y. 10022. Published simultaneously in Canada by Fitzhenry & Whiteside Limited, Toronto.

First edition.

Type Design: John Lynch

Library of Congress Cataloging-in-Publication Data
Stephens, Vanessa.
  The classic book of baby names.

  1. Names, Personal—United States.   2. Names,
Personal—English.   I. Conner, Mona.   II. Title.
CS2377.S58   1988   929.4′0973   87-46172
ISBN 0-06-016000-4

88 89 90 91 92 10 9 8 7 6 5 4 3 2 1

This book is dedicated to our child

_____
(NAME)

whose name we chose because

_____

_____

_____

_____

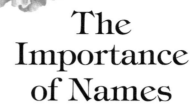

The Importance of Names

The first—and the most lasting—gift you'll ever give your baby is his or her name. Throughout your child's life, this name will reflect your tastes, your and your child's background, and your sensibilities.

When choosing a name, it's important to remember how lasting your choice really is. If you're attracted to a "cute" combination of first and last names—punning or rhyming names, for instance—remember that this is a name your child will have *all* of his or her life, not just through babyhood. "Made-up" names—combinations of first and last initials, place names, names commemorating events—should be avoided for the same reasons.

This book is dedicated to the idea that a given name can enhance a person's life, that the original meaning of the name, the legacy of the people who have borne the name, and the euphony of the name will give pleasure and a sense of history. Your careful and thoughtful reasons for choosing a name, as well as the name itself, are part of the inheritance you pass on to your child.

The combination of given and surname should be pleasing to both the eye and the ear. Strive for a harmonious balance between

the syllables of the first name and the last name. Some of this will depend on your own taste: one-syllable first and last names will sound snappy and clean-cut, while a three-syllable first and a three-syllable last name will sound either delightfully old-fashioned or ponderous. Say your child's name out loud and write it down to see if you enjoy it. You should think, too, about the nicknames derived from the name you have chosen, for, regardless of your wishes, your child will likely be known by one of them, particularly during childhood.

Middle names, again, are a matter of personal choice. Many parents prefer to use a familial surname as a middle name. Others, who have no such appropriate family name to pass on, choose a second name along the same principles as the first.

Because this book focuses specifically on the enduring and the classic, it deliberately does not include many of the trendy names popular today. What is trendy today will, in our opinion, sound merely tacky ten years hence—and a name should carry its own weight far longer than that. The names included here have one thing in common: they have all stood the test of history.

_____
MOTHER

Our Baby's
Family Tree
of Names

_____
FATHER

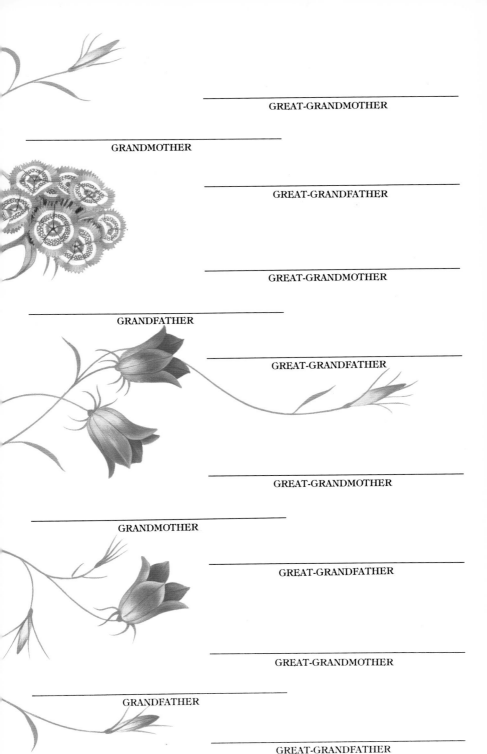

GREAT-GRANDMOTHER

GRANDMOTHER

GREAT-GRANDFATHER

GREAT-GRANDMOTHER

GRANDFATHER

GREAT-GRANDFATHER

GREAT-GRANDMOTHER

GRANDMOTHER

GREAT-GRANDFATHER

GREAT-GRANDMOTHER

GRANDFATHER

GREAT-GRANDFATHER

A good name
is better than precious
ointment.

Ecclesiastes 7:1

GIRLS' NAMES

A

Abigail From the Hebrew name *Avigayil,* meaning "source of joy." Among the bearers of the name was Abigail Adams, beloved wife of John Adams, second President of the United States. Variants: *Abbe, Abbey, Abby, Gail.*

Adrienne French feminine form of a Latin place-name (Hadria) meaning "black earth." Variants: *Adria, Adrian, Adrien.*

Agatha From the Greek, meaning "good."

Agnes From the Greek and Latin, meaning "lamb," symbolizing chastity and purity.

Ainslee From the Scottish, meaning "one's own meadow."

Alana Feminine form of *Alan,* from the Celtic, meaning "harmony, peace" or "fair, handsome." Variants: *Alanna, Allana, Alina, Lana, Lane.*

Alexandra Feminine form of *Alexander,* from the Greek, meaning "protector of man." This elegant name, popular with Europe's royal families, has yielded some beautiful national variants: *Alessandra* (Italian), *Alexandria,* and *Alexandrina* (Russian). Other variants: *Alexa, Alexia, Alexis, Alexei, Sandra.*

Alice From the French, meaning "noble," or the Greek, meaning "truth." A popular name that became even more so with the publication in 1865 of *Alice's Adventures in Wonderland.* The charm of this name lies in its simplicity and its British overtones. Variants: *Ali, Alie, Alix, Alyse, Alissa, Alison.*

Alison, Alyson "Son of Alice."

Allegra From the Latin, meaning "sprightly, cheerful." A musical name in both sound and meaning, with a touch of the exotic.

Althea From the Greek, meaning "healing." A stately name.

Amanda From the Latin, meaning "beloved"; it shares its root with *Amy*, but where Amy is pretty, Amanda is elegant.

Amelia From the German, meaning "striving."

Amity From the Latin, meaning "friendship." For other names referring to virtues, see *Charity, Faith, Hope.* A legacy of America's Puritan roots.

Amy French, from the Latin, meaning "the beloved." Variants: *Aimée, Amata, Amia.*

Anais A variant of *Anne.*

Anastasia From the Greek, meaning "resurrection." Name of one of the Romanoff princesses. A classic name that bears little relationship to the modern derivative *Stacey.*

Andrea A feminine form of *Andrew,* from the Greek, meaning "strong, courageous."

Angela From the Latin, meaning "angelic."

Angelica A variant form of *Angela.*

Ann, Anne A French form of the Hebrew *Hannah,* meaning "gracious." A name popular with royalty. Variants: *Ani, Anni, Annie, Annette, Anita, Nan, Nancy, Nanette, Nina.*

Annabella, Annabelle A compound form of *Anna*, meaning "gracious," and *Bella*, meaning "beautiful." Variant: *Annabel*.

Anthea From the Greek, meaning "flowery." Related in meaning are *Fleur*, from the French, and *Flora*, from the Latin.

Antoinette The French feminine form of *Antony*, from the Greek "flourishing" and the Latin "worthy of praise." The form favored by the English, *Antonia*, is perhaps the most elegant.

Arden Both an Anglo-Saxon place-name and a name from the Latin, meaning "a flame" or "passionate." Arden is endowed with Shakespearian overtones.

Ariadne From Greek mythology, the daughter of the sun god. Variants: *Ariane, Arianna*.

Ariel From the Hebrew, meaning "lioness of God." Through its association with Shakespeare, it has Anglo-Saxon overtones as well.

Astera From the Greek, meaning "star." Its Persian equivalent, *Esther*, is associated with the goddess of the moon in Phoenician mythology and is also the name of a biblical heroine. Variants: *Asteria, Astra*.

Audrey From the Old English, meaning "noble strength."

Augusta Feminine form of *Augustus*. From the Latin, meaning "revered." A formal name little used in modern times.

Barbara From the Greek and Latin, meaning "strange." While Barbara has noble antecedents—a number of saints have borne the name—the often appalling nicknames (Babs, Bobbi, Barbi, and so on) make it a hard choice for a first name.

Beatrice From the Latin, meaning "one who brings happiness." A name with a lovely connotation and a fine literary pedigree—Shakespeare's heroine in *Much Ado About Nothing* and Dante's beloved in *The Divine Comedy*—and a royal one as well. Variants: *Bice, Beatrix, Bettrys*.

Beryl From the Persian and Arabic, meaning "crystal."

Beth Properly a nickname, though popular of late as a given name. See *Elizabeth*.

C

Camille French, from the Latin, meaning "servant of the temple." A name that became popular during the eighteenth-century vogue for classical names (the original form, *Camilla*, appears in *The Aeneid*).

Candace From the Greek, meaning "incandescent," and the Latin, meaning "pure"; in the Bible the name of the Ethiopian queen. While the nickname Candy is vulgar, the longer variant forms—*Candice, Candide,* and *Canida*—are elegant. The English *Candida* (see George Bernard Shaw's play of the same name) is especially lovely.

Carol(e) Either from the Gaelic, meaning "song," or a short form of *Caroline.*

Caroline The feminine form of the Anglo-Saxon *Charles,* meaning "manly." A name popular since the time of the English Stuart kings and made more so when King George II married his queen, Caroline. Variants: *Carolina, Carol, Carole, Carolyn.* Nicknames: Carey, Carly, Carrie, Carry, Cassie.

Cassandra From the Greek, meaning "helper of men." In Greek mythology Apollo bestowed the gift of prophecy upon Cassandra but, in the end, decreed that no one should heed her. The sound of the name, though, is lovely.

Catherine From the Greek, meaning "pure." A beautiful and classic name with literary and royal antecedents, among them Catherine the Great of Russia and the heroine of Emily Brontë's *Wuthering Heights,* Catherine Earnshaw. Some of the national variations are appealing as well: *Catherina* (Italian), *Katrini* (Slavic), *Caren* and *Karen* (Scandinavian), *Caitlin* (Welsh). The English *Kate* is most pleasing.

Cecilia From the Latin, meaning "blind." St. Cecilia was the patron saint of music, and during the sixteenth, seventeenth, and eighteenth centuries, poets, including John Dryden and Alexander Pope, dedicated poems to her. The variants, *Cecily, Cecile, Cicely,* and *Celia,* are elegant as well.

Charity From the Latin *caritas,* meaning "affection." A popular Puritan name that has largely fallen out of favor in modern times.

Charlotte French, a feminine form of Charlot (*Charles*). See *Caroline.*

Christiana From the Latin, meaning "follower of Christ." The prettiest and most popular variant is the English *Christina,* although the French version, *Christine,* and the Slavic *Kirsten* are also lovely.

Clara From the Latin, meaning "bright." To many a modern ear, Clara may sound plain, but its variants—*Claira, Clarice, Clarinda,* and *Clarissa*—are good names to consider. *Larissa* is a short form of Clarissa.

Clarice See *Clara.*

Claudia From the Latin, meaning "lame."

Clemence Feminine form of *Clement,* from the Latin, meaning "merciful." A name largely abandoned in modern times.

Constance From the Latin, meaning "faithful." A stately first name (like the form preferred in the nineteenth century, *Constantia*), although its nickname, Connie, is less desirable.

Consuelo From the Latin, meaning "consolation." A beautiful but old-fashioned name.

Cordelia Celtic, the name of the youngest daughter in Shakespeare's *King Lear*.

Cornelia From the Latin, the feminine form of *Cornelius*.

Courtney Originally an Old French place-name, meaning "he who frequents the king's court." In terms of first-name usage, not strictly a classic name, although a pretty one.

Cybil See *Sibyl*.

Cynthia From the Greek, the goddess of the moon. (In Roman myth she was named Diana.) During the English Renaissance, Queen Elizabeth I was addressed as Cynthia by the courtier poets Ben Jonson, Walter Raleigh, and Edmund Spenser. *Cindy* as a nickname is unfortunate.

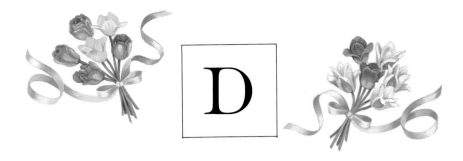

D

Dana A variant of *Dan*. From the Hebrew, meaning "God is my judge." Used as a masculine name from the nineteenth century on, it became popular as a feminine name in the twentieth century.

Danielle The feminine form of *Daniel*, from the Hebrew, meaning "God is my judge." Variants: *Daniela, Daniele.*

Daphne From the Greek, meaning "laurel tree." In Greek mythology a nymph pursued by Apollo is changed into a laurel tree to avoid his pursuit. A fashionable name in the nineteenth century.

Deborah From the Hebrew, meaning "a bee." In the Bible Deborah was a prophet or judge of Israel. The nicknames *Debbi* or *Debby* are suitable only for the smallest of children.

Deirdre Irish; in legend a beautiful princess. The name was made popular by William Butler Yeats's *Deirdre* and John Millington Synge's *Deirdre of the Sorrows*, plays that testify to the name's strong Irish roots.

Diana From the Latin, meaning "divine"; in Roman times the goddess of the hunt and the moon. The current Princess of Wales is doubtless the most visible public figure to bear the name. Variants include *Diane* and *Dione*.

Dorothy From the Greek for "gift of God," a meaning clearer in its original form, *Dorothea*.

Edith From the Anglo-Saxon and Teutonic, meaning "prospering." A popular name in the nineteenth century, borne by some very distinguished women: novelist Edith Wharton, classical scholar Edith Hamilton, and actress Dame Edith Evans.

Elaine French form of *Helen*.

Eleanor German form of *Helen*.

Elizabeth From the Hebrew, meaning "God's oath." A truly classic name that has graced the mother of John the Baptist, as well as saints and queens, among them Elizabeth I of England. As a formal name, it is almost unmatched in its beauty. Among the pet forms, one might consider Bess, Beth, Bettina, Eliza, Liza, Lizbeth, and Lizzie.

Ellen See *Helen*.

Emily The feminine form of the Latin name *Aemilus*, or derived from the German, both meaning "striving" or "ambitious." A very popular nineteenth-century name. See also *Amelia*.

Emma Origin unclear. Perhaps connected to *Emily* or a Teutonic name. The name of a daughter of Charlemagne, it is more commonly associated with two novels, Gustave Flaubert's *Madame Bovary* and Jane Austen's *Emma*.

Enid From the Celtic, meaning "pure." In Arthurian legend, Enid, the wife of Geraint, is noble and true; Tennyson's *Idylls of the King* helped popularize the name.

Esther From the Persian, meaning "star"; in the Bible the Persian name of the Jewish queen who saved her people.

Emily, that fairer was to see
than is the lily upon his stalk green.
Geoffrey Chaucer

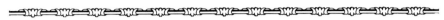

Eugenia From the Greek, meaning "nobility." The French form, *Eugénie,* made popular during the nineteenth century by the Empress Eugénie, wife of Louis Napoleon, is also pretty.

Eve From the Hebrew, meaning "life"; related to *Zoe,* originally the Greek word used in Biblical translation. A variant form of the name is *Eva.*

Evelyn From the Celtic, meaning "pleasant." The poet Robert Browning (1812–1889) sang the name's praises in "Evelyn Hope." Evelyn is also a masculine name.

Faith From the Latin, meaning "to trust." A Puritan favorite.

Fay From the Old French, meaning "fidelity," or a shortened version of *Faith*.

Felicia From the Latin, meaning "happiness." Felicitas was the goddess of good luck. *Felice* is a variant.

Fidelity From the Latin, meaning "faithfulness." One of the virtue names, less popular today than its cousins *Faith* and *Hope*. *Fidelia* is a variant form.

Flora From the Latin, meaning "flower." Victorian in feeling, Flora has a host of variants, among them *Florence* and *Floris*.

Florence From the Latin, meaning "flowering." Originally both a masculine and a feminine name, it became identified as primarily a feminine name in the nineteenth century. The nickname *Flo* is vulgar.

Frances The feminine version of *Francis*, meaning "Frenchman."

Frederica The feminine form of *Frederic*, from the High German, meaning "peaceful ruler."

G

Gabriel(1)a Feminine form of *Gabriel*, from the Hebrew, meaning "man of God." A name more popular abroad than in the United States.

Gail see *Abigail*.

Georgia The feminine form of *George*, from the Greek, meaning "farmer."

Gillian See *Julia*.

Gloria From the Latin, meaning "glory."

Grace From the Latin, meaning "grace." A Puritan name that has declined in popularity but is worthy of revival.

Guenevere, Guinevere From the Celtic, meaning "white" (gwen) and perhaps "wave." Although rarely used today, it was a popular nineteenth-century name, partly because of the revival of interest in Arthurian legend. (Guenevere was King Arthur's queen.) *Jennifer* is the modern-day English variant.

Gwendolen, Gwendolyn From the Welsh, meaning "white-browed."

H

Hannah From the Hebrew, meaning "gracious." In the Bible the mother of the prophet Samuel. See *Ann*.

Harriet The feminine form of *Harry*, from the High German, meaning "home ruler."

Helen From the Greek, meaning "torch" or "light." Perhaps the most famous bearer of the name was Helen of Troy whose face "launched a thousand ships." Classic variants include *Elaine, Eleanor, Ellen, Leonora, Helene, Elena,* and *Helena.*

Henrietta Feminine form of *Henry*, from the Old High German, meaning "home ruler." *Henriette* is the French variant form.

Hilary From the Latin, meaning "cheerful." Also a masculine name.

Holly From the Old English, an evergreen shrub bearing red berries, once considered a talisman of good luck.

Honor, Honora From the Latin, meaning "honorable." A popular Puritan virtue name. In modern times it has become less popular than its variant forms, *Nora* and *Noreen.*

Hope From the Old English, meaning "faith." A favorite name among the Puritans.

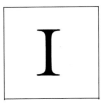

I

Irene From the Greek, meaning "peace."

Isabel A variant of *Elizabeth.* An important name among the royal families of Europe in its national variants, *Isabelle* (French) and *Isabella* (Spanish).

Ivy From the Teutonic, meaning "clinging." This name, along with other plant and flower names, enjoyed a vogue at the turn of the century.

Jacqueline French feminine form of *Jacob*, from the Hebrew, meaning "to supplant." *Jacoba* is the closer Latinate form, while *Jocelin* is a Germanic variant. The shortened forms *Jackie* and *Jacqui* should never be used as first names and should be avoided as nicknames.

Jane From the Hebrew, meaning "God is gracious"; the feminine form of *John;* a very old name whose popularity—as well as that of its variants (*Johanna, Joanna, Joan, Jean*)—has ebbed and flowed.

Jasmin From the Persian, meaning "jasmine." One of the flower names popular at the end of the nineteenth century.

Jennifer See *Guenevere.*

Jill See *Julia.*

Joan, Joanna, Johanna See *Jane.*

Jocelin A variation of *Jacoba.* See *Jacqueline.*

Judith From the Hebrew, meaning "object of praise." In Genesis the name of Esau's first wife; in the Apocrypha Judith seduces and slays the Assyrian commander.

Julia Feminine form of *Julius*, from the Latin, perhaps meaning "soft hair." A beautiful name whose variants—*Julian, Juliana,* and *Gillian*—are equally pleasing. *Juliet* is a diminutive of Julia while Gillian was the source for the shortened form, Jill.

Justine Feminine form of *Justin*, from the Latin, meaning "just."

K·L

Karen A variant of *Catherine*.

Katharine, Katherine see *Catherine*.

Kirsten See *Christiana*.

Laura From the Latin, meaning "laurel." A name popularized by the Italian poet Petrarch. *Laurel* is a stately variant, while *Lauren*—perhaps because of its lilting sound—is more popular.

Leah From the Hebrew, meaning "weary." *Lea* is the French variant.

Lesley, Leslie From the Old English, meaning "meadow"; probably originated as a place-name. Its use as a feminine name is relatively recent, and indeed in Britain, Lesley is primarily a masculine name.

Letitia From the Latin, meaning "joy."

Lilian From the Latin, meaning "lily." *Lily, Lilly,* and *Lillian* became popular flower names at the end of the nineteenth century.

Lisa A variant of *Elizabeth*.

Louise French feminine form of *Louis*, from the Old German, meaning "famous warrior." For centuries a very popular name among royalty whose variant form *Louisa* was further popularized by the success of Louisa May Alcott's novels.

Lucia From the Latin, meaning "to shine." The English form, *Lucinda,* is a pleasant alternative.

Madeleine French form of *Magdalene*, from the Hebrew, meaning "high tower."

Margaret From the Greek, meaning "pearl." A classic name that has endured and been borne by countless women of royal lineage. It yields many beautiful national variations, among them *Margo, Margot, Marguerite, Margery, Marjorie, Margiad,* and *Megan*. While the formal name is elegant, some of the nicknames—Peggy, Maggie—are less so.

Margery A variant form of *Margaret*.

Margo(t) A variant form of *Margaret*.

Maria, Marie See *Mary*.

Marian(ne) French variant of *Marie*, as is *Marion*. Extremely popular in the Middle Ages, the name is most often associated with the Robin Hood legend. See *Mary*.

Martha From the Aramaic, meaning "a lady." A biblical name, both elegant and stylish. Two variants to consider are *Marthe* (French) and *Marta* (Italian).

Mary From the Hebrew, meaning "bitterness" or "sorrow." In the Bible the mother of Jesus. A simple name that resonates with history, borne by commoner and royalty alike. Among the national variants are *Marie* (German, French); *Marion, Maron, Mariette* (French); *Maria* (Latin, Italian, Spanish); *Miriam* (Hebrew); *Marya* (Slavic); *Maureen, Maura, Moira* (Irish); and *Mariele* (Dutch).

Megan See *Margaret*.

I have a passion for the name of "Mary,"
For once it was a magic sound to me,
And still it half calls up the realms of fairy.
Where I beheld what never was to be.

George Gordon, Lord Byron

Melanie From the Greek, meaning "dark." The name of two saints, as well as the soft-spoken epitome of kindness in Margaret Mitchell's *Gone with the Wind.*

Melissa From the Greek, meaning "bee." A very popular and pretty name.

Melody From the Greek, meaning "song."

Meredith Origin unclear. Perhaps from the Welsh, meaning "sea protector." Primarily a masculine name.

Michaela The feminine form of *Michael,* from the Hebrew, meaning "who is like the Lord?" The French variants *Michele* and *Michelle* are perhaps more feminine sounding.

Michele See *Michaela.*

Millicent From the Old German, meaning "strength." An old-fashioned name that merits revival.

Milly Nickname for *Millicent* and *Mildred.*

Miranda From the Latin, meaning "admirable." A name made famous—and perhaps invented—by William Shakespeare in *The Tempest.*

Moira See *Mary.*

Morgan From the Welsh; primarily a masculine name. Variant: *Morgana.*

Nancy See *Ann.*

Naomi From the Hebrew, meaning "pleasant."

Natalie From the French, meaning "to be born."

Nicola Italian feminine form of *Nicholas*, from the Greek, meaning "victory of the people."

Nicole(tte) French feminine form of *Nicholas.* See *Nicola.*

Nina See *Ann.*

Noel(le) From the French, meaning "birthday of Christ." More properly a masculine name, although it is traditionally given to children born on Christmas day.

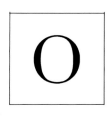

Octavia From the Latin, meaning "the eight." A very formal name.

Olive From the Latin, meaning "olive tree," the symbol of peace. *Olivia* is the preferred, more elegant form; Livia is a lovely nickname.

Ophelia From the Greek, meaning "to help." Shakespeare's *Hamlet* popularized the name.

P

Page More properly a surname.

Paloma From the Spanish, meaning "dove."

Pamela A distinguished name that was invented by Sir Philip Sidney, courtier to England's Queen Elizabeth I, and used in his *Arcadia* (1590). Samuel Richardson's novel *Pamela* brought the name into vogue again in the mid–eighteenth century, and it has rarely been out of favor since.

Patience From the Latin, meaning either "patient" or "long-suffering." One of the virtue names, like *Charity* and *Hope*.

Patricia The feminine form of *Patrick*, from the Latin, meaning "of noble birth." Trish, Patty, and Patsy are common nicknames.

Paula The feminine form of *Paul*, from the Latin, meaning "small." *Pauline* is the French variant.

Penelope From the Greek, meaning "weaver." The name of Odysseus' wife in Homer's *Odyssey*, and anyone who has read this magnificent poem will understand the connotation of the name. The nickname *Penny*, alas, conveys none of Penelope's grandeur.

Petra The feminine form of *Peter*, from the Greek, meaning "rock." An elegant name that to the American ear sounds very English; it is indeed a popular name in Britain, as is *Philippa*.

Philippa The feminine form of *Philip*, from the Greek, meaning "lover of horses." The name is less commonly bestowed in the United States than in England.

> Patience is a flower that grows
> not in every garden.
>
> James Howell

Phoebe From the Greek, meaning "shining one." In Greek myth the goddess of the moon.

Portia From the Latin, meaning "pig." Originally a Roman family name. Although its meaning is unfortunate, the name has both historical and literary grandeur: Portia was Brutus' wife and the heroine of Shakespeare's *Merchant of Venice*.

Priscilla From the Latin, meaning "old." A biblical name whose American roots reach back to the Puritan era, most notably in the figure of Priscilla Alden and her appearance in Henry Wadsworth Longfellow's "The Courtship of Miles Standish."

Prudence From the Latin, meaning "wise." A virtue name, favored by the Puritan forefathers.

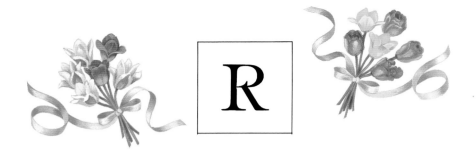

Rachel From the Hebrew, meaning "female sheep." In the Bible the mother of Jacob.

Raphaela The feminine form of *Raphael*, from the Hebrew, meaning "God has healed."

Rebecca From the Hebrew, meaning "yoke." In the Bible Rebecca was the wife of Isaac and the mother of Jacob and Esau, and in literature she was the heroine of Sir Walter Scott's *Ivanhoe*. William Thackeray's unpleasant heroine in *Vanity Fair* was named Becky Sharp; he rightly judged the nickname as prickly as his character.

Regan See *Regina*.

Regina From the Latin, meaning "queen." *Regan* is a variant form.

Renata From the Latin, meaning "reborn."

Rene(e) A variant form of *Renata*.

Roberta The feminine form of *Robert*, from the Teutonic, meaning "of shining fame." The nickname *Bobbi* is less suitable.

Rosalia Origin and meaning uncertain. Perhaps from the French, via the Latin, or from the Irish. *Rosalie* is the French form.

Rosalind From the Latin, meaning "pretty rose." A name popularized by the heroine in William Shakespeare's *As You Like It*. Variant forms include *Roselyn* and *Roslyn*.

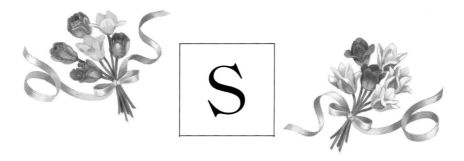

Samantha From the Aramaic, meaning "the listener." A very attractive name that has become rather trendy.

Sara(h) From the Hebrew, meaning "princess." In the Bible Sarah was the mother of Isaac. A distinguished name, borne by many luminaries, among them two of the stage's most distinguished actresses, Sarah Bernhardt and Sarah Siddons.

Sarai The original form of *Sarah*.

Seraphina From the Hebrew, meaning "angel."

Shannon The feminine form of *Sean*, itself the Irish variant of *John*.

Sibyl From the Greek, meaning "prophetess." Sibyl is the spelling preferred by anglophiles. Variant: *Cybil*.

Sophia From the Greek, meaning "wisdom." Henry Fielding's heroine in his novel *Tom Jones* accounted for some of the name's popularity. Among the national variants are *Sophy* (English), *Sophie* (French), *Sonja* and *Sonya* (Russian).

Stephanie The feminine form of *Stephen*, from the Greek, meaning "a crown." As a masculine name, favored by many saints.

Susan From the Hebrew, meaning "lily." Among the variant forms are *Susanna*, *Susannah*, and *Susanne*. Not an unusual name, but a pretty one.

Sylvia From the Latin, meaning "forest." Variants include *Silve*, *Silvana*, and *Sylvana*.

T·U

Tabitha From the Aramaic, meaning "gazelle."

Tatiana From the Russian. In Shakespeare's *A Midsummer Night's Dream* the queen of the fairies is Titania, which may be a variant, along with *Tanya*.

Temperance From the Latin, meaning "measured." A virtue name more popular in the Puritan era.

Teresa See *Theresa*.

Tess See *Theresa*.

Theodora The feminine form of Theodore, from the Greek, meaning "God's gifts." The name of the Byzantine empress who, with the Emperor Justinian, ruled in the sixth century. See also *Dorothy*.

Theresa From the Greek. Among the variant forms are *Therese* (French) and *Terry* and *Tracy* (English). *Tess* has a particularly English sound, doubtless because of Thomas Hardy's novel *Tess of the D'Urbervilles*.

Tracey, Tracy See *Theresa*.

Una From the Latin, meaning "the one." In Ireland the variants *Ona* and *Oona* are popular. Una is also the name of the character symbolizing truth in Edmund Spenser's *Faerie Queene*.

Ursula From the Latin, meaning "little bear."

V·Z

Valeria From the Latin, meaning "to be strong." *Valerie* is the French form.

Vanessa A beautiful name invented by Jonathan Swift in honor of Hester Vanhomrigh, whose nickname was Essie.

Verity From the Latin, meaning "truth." A virtue name, akin to Verita. The variant *Vera* is less pleasing.

Victoria The feminine form of *Victor*, from the Latin, meaning "victorious." The most famous bearer of this distinguished and elegant name is doubtless the queen of Britain and Ireland (1837–1901), wife of Albert, whose name is an eponym for her era. The national variants of the name, *Victoire* (French) and *Vittoria* (Italian), are also attractive, although the pet form *Vicky* is far less pleasing and isn't entirely appropriate as a first name.

Virginia From the Latin, meaning "pure." A name with roots in the New World. The colony Virginia was named in honor of Elizabeth I of England, the Virgin Queen, and the first colonial baby was named Virginia Dare. Ginger is a nickname and should not be used as a given name.

Vivian From the Latin, meaning "alive." In Arthurian legend Vivian was an enchantress. *Vivien* and *Vivienne* are the French forms.

Zoe From the Greek, meaning "life."

A good name
is rather to be chosen
than great riches.

Proverbs 22:1

BOYS'
NAMES

A

Aaron From the Hebrew, meaning "light" or "mountain." In the Bible Aaron was the brother of Moses.

Abraham From the Hebrew, meaning "father of a multitude." Abraham Lincoln, sixteenth president of the United States, is one of the most distinguished bearers of the name and, of course, contributed to its popularity.

Adam From the Hebrew, meaning "earth." In some sense, the *first* first name.

Adrian See *Hadrian*.

Alan From the Celtic, meaning "handsome."

Alastair The Scottish form of *Alexander*.

Albert From the Old German, meaning "noble" or "bright." A name that has been borne by royalty and luminaries from all walks of life. The name became very popular in England after the marriage of Victoria to Prince Albert in 1840.

Alexander From the Greek, meaning "protector of man." A name that has been esteemed since the time of Alexander the Great. Among the distinguished national variants are *Alexandre* (French), *Alessandro* (Italian), *Aleksandr* (Russian), *Alasdair* and *Alastair* (Gaelic). Among the nicer nicknames are Alec, Alex, Sander, Sandy, and Sasha.

Alfred From the Old English, meaning "elf counsel." The ninth-century English king Alfred the Great drove back the Danish invaders and left as his legacy one of England's most popular names.

Algernon From the French, meaning "with mustache." A popular name in the nineteenth century.

Allen See Alan.

Ambrose From the Greek, meaning "immortal."

Andrew From the Greek, meaning "manly." The Apostle Andrew is the patron saint of Scotland and Russia, which accounts in part for the name's extraordinary and enduring popularity around the world. Among the variant forms are *Andre* (French), *Andreas* (Latin, German, and Dutch), *Anders* (Danish), and *Andrei* (Russian).

Angus From the Gaelic, meaning "unique." In Irish and Celtic myth Angus was the god of love.

Anson From the Anglo-Saxon, meaning "son of Hans [John]."

Ant(h)ony From the Latin, meaning "praiseworthy" or "priceless." Originally the name of a Roman family, whose most famous member was Marcus Antonius. Tony is the nickname.

Archibald From the Anglo-Saxon, meaning "very bold."

Arnold From the Old German, meaning "eagle-power." A very popular name in Europe in all its national variations, *Armand, Arnoldo,* and *Arend* among them.

Arthur From various sources. The most famous bearer of the name is certainly the legendary English king who presided over the knights of the Round Table and has been celebrated in literature for centuries. Art is a pleasing nickname.

Ashley From the Old English, meaning "meadow of ash trees." A lovely name that deserves to be associated with something other than *Gone with the Wind*. Although traditionally a masculine name, Ashley is increasingly bestowed on girls as well.

August(us) From the Latin, meaning "exalted." A name that originated as a title given the first Roman emperor by the Roman senate. An appealing and eminently classic shorter form of English origin is *Austin* (or *Austen*).

Austen, Austin See *August(us)*.

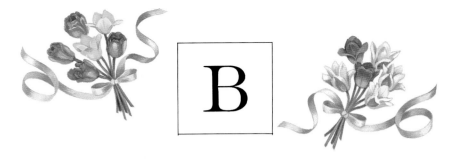

B

Bartholomew From the Aramaic, meaning "son of Talmai." One of the twelve Apostles in the Bible.

Basil From the Greek, meaning "kingly."

Benedict From the Latin, meaning "blessed." The English variant *Bennet(t)* is also very appealing.

Benjamin From the Hebrew, meaning "son of my right hand." A classic name, borne by the American Revolutionary patriot Benjamin Harrison, signer of the Declaration of Independence, and the inventor and statesman Benjamin Franklin.

Bernard From the Old German, meaning "stern bear."

Bertram From the Old German, meaning "illustrious."

Blair From the Celtic, originally a place-name and more properly a surname.

Bradley From the Old English, meaning "meadow." Brad is a nickname.

Brian From the Celtic, meaning "strong." An alternate spelling is *Bryan.*

Burgess From the Middle English, meaning "citizen of a borough."

Byron Origin unclear. A name that owes its existence to the popularity of the English poet George, Lord Byron, but in fact is an elegant first name.

Caleb From the Hebrew, meaning "faithful." A name evocative of America's Puritan roots.

Calvin From the Latin, meaning "bald." Calvin became a given name in honor of the Protestant reformer John Calvin. Cal is the short form.

Cameron From the Scottish, meaning "crooked nose."

Carl See *Charles*.

Carter From the Anglo-Saxon, meaning "cart driver." A name that has its origins in a humble occupation but which, in the twentieth century, is both elegant and distinguished (a good example of progress!).

Cecil From the Latin, meaning "blind." A very popular name in Britain, though rarely given in America.

Cedric An invented name—like *Vanessa*—this one by Sir Walter Scott for a character in *Ivanhoe*. Associated by most Americans, for this and other reasons, with things English. (It was, after all, Little Lord Fauntleroy's first name.)

Charles From the Anglo-Saxon, meaning "strong." A name that resounds with a sense of history, borne by countless crowned heads, from the Emperor of France, Charlemagne, to the Stuart kings to the current Prince of Wales. Its national variants are *Carl* (English), *Karl* (German), and *Carlo(s)* (Romance languages).

Christian From the Latin, meaning "a Christian." An elegant name that has lost its popularity.

For thee, my gentlehearted Charles, to whom
No sound is dissonant which tells of life . . .

Samuel Taylor Coleridge

Christopher From the Greek, meaning "bearer of Christ." The meaning of the name is directly linked to Saint Christopher, who carried Christ across a river. A beautiful name but extremely popular of late: those seeking to stand out in a crowd, beware. Chris is a very common nickname.

Clarence From the Latin, meaning "clear." A pleasantly old-fashioned name.

Clifford From the Old English; a place-name meaning "a crossing near the cliff."

Clive From the Old English; a place-name meaning "a steep bank." Variant forms: *Cleveland, Clifford*. Clive sounds very English to the American ear.

Colin See *Nicholas*.

Corliss See *Charles*.

Cornelius From the Latin, meaning "cornell tree." A distinguished Roman family name that became popular in the Low Countries and was imported into America by Dutch settlers. Cornelius Vanderbilt, the railroad magnate, displays the name's heritage well.

Craig From the Celtic, meaning "crag."

Cyril From the Greek, meaning "lord." A name more popular in Britain than in the United States. Variants include *Kiril* and *Kyril*.

Dana See *Daniel*.

Daniel From the Hebrew, meaning "God is my judge." In the Bible the prophet who escaped from the lion's den, where he was thrown for disobedience to Darius, the king of Persia. Dan is a fine nickname.

David From the Hebrew, meaning "beloved." In the Bible the second king of Israel. An old and much-loved name.

Davis A form of *David*, meaning "son of David."

Den(n)is The French form of the Greek *Dionysus*, referring to the god of wine. *Denys* is a variant spelling.

Derek Origin unclear, perhaps from the Teutonic; probably a pet form of *Theodoric*. See *Theodore*.

Desmond From the Gaelic. Originally a clan name and place-name meaning "South Munster."

Dirk Origin uncertain. Probably related to *Derek* in that it derives from *Theodoric*.

Donald From the Gaelic, meaning "proud ruler." The nickname *Don* is preferable to the more juvenile *Donny*.

Douglas From the Scottish, meaning "dark water." A famous Scottish clan bore this name, after settling near a dark river.

Duncan From the Celtic, meaning "brown warrior." In Scotland a royal name.

Edgar From the Anglo-Saxon, meaning "felicitous spear."

Edmund From the Anglo-Saxon, meaning "happy protector." A variant spelling is *Edmond*.

Edward From the Anglo-Saxon, meaning "happy protector." The name of the Saxon kings as well as eight kings of England. Its national variants are equally regal: *Edouard* (French), *Eduard* (German), and *Edvard* (Scandinavian). Ed and Eddy are common nicknames, as is Ned.

Edwin From the Anglo-Saxon, meaning "happy friend."

Elijah From the Hebrew, meaning "the Lord is my God." In the Bible one of the Hebrew prophets. The national variants of the name are popular and, in many cases, noble: *Elia* (Greek), *Elie* (French), *Eliot(t)* and *Ellis* (English).

Elliot(t), Ellis See *Elijah*.

Eric From the Norse, meaning "ruler." *Erie* and *Erich* are variant forms.

Ernest From the Old German, meaning "steadfast" or "resolute." Primarily a German name until its introduction into England in the late eighteenth century by the Hanoverian dynasty.

Ethan From the Hebrew, meaning "firm." A name that has American roots, not only in the figure of legendary patriot Ethan Allen (1738–89) but also in American writer Edith Wharton's *Ethan Frome*.

Evan The Welsh form of *John*.

Felix From the Latin, meaning "happy." Four popes have borne the name, as well as a number of saints.

Ferdinand From the Teutonic, meaning "adventuring life." The name—clearly appropriate—of the king of Spain under whose flag Columbus set forth.

Francis From the Latin, meaning "Frenchman." Originally a name referring to one who spoke French; also the name of an early French king and Saint Francis of Assisi. Frank is the nickname.

Franklin From the Teutonic, meaning "freeholder." Originally a surname; only in the United States—where it was popularized by Benjamin Franklin—is it used as a first name.

Frederick From the Old German, meaning "peaceful ruler." A name of distinction, borne by Frederick II of Prussia and Frederic Chopin, among others.

G

Gabriel From the Hebrew, meaning "God is mighty." In the Bible one of the seven archangels, the herald of good news.

Gareth See *Garth*.

Garth From the Anglo-Saxon, meaning "firm spear."

Gary Origin unclear. Either from the Anglo-Saxon, or from a Celtic place-name.

Geoffrey The French form of *Godfrey*. *Jeffrey* is an alternate spelling.

George From the Greek, meaning "farmer." A name that has graced the heads of many, from the famed killer of the dragon (St. George) to the king of England during the American Revolution and the first president of the United States, George Washington, to the great American composer George Gershwin.

Gerald From the Teutonic, meaning "firm spear."

Gerard A variation of *Gerald*.

Gilbert From the Old German, meaning "bright pledge."

Giles From the Greek, meaning "shield bearer." A name popular among anglophiles.

Godfrey From the Germanic, meaning "God's peace."

Gregory From the Greek, meaning "watchful." Sixteen popes have borne this name, accounting for a great deal of its popularity.

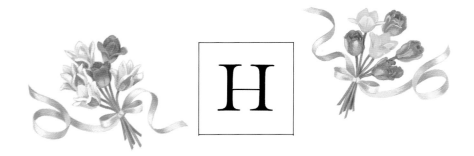

Hadrian From the Latin, meaning "black earth." *Adrian* is a shortened form.

Harold From the Old English, meaning "army leader." Harold was the last of the Saxon kings, celebrated in literature by such diverse voices as Alfred, Lord Tennyson, and Sir Edward George Bulwer-Lytton. Hal is a nickname.

Harry An English form of *Henry*, itself used as a proper name. The Prince and Princess of Wales' son bears this name.

Henry From the Old High German, meaning "home rule." The list of famous men who share this name is too long to enumerate. Hank is the least elegant of the nicknames associated with Henry, while Hal is the most pleasant.

Herbert From the Anglo-Saxon, meaning "bright ruler."

Herman From the Old High German, meaning "soldier."

Heywood From the Anglo-Saxon, a place-name meaning "a woody enclosure." Variant: *Haywood*.

Hilary From the Latin, meaning "cheerful." In the United States this is largely thought of as a feminine name, though not in England.

Hiram From the Hebrew, meaning "exalted." A biblical name that has fallen out of favor.

Horace From the Latin, perhaps meaning "hour" but definitely the name of a Roman *gens*, the *Horatii*. The name is resonant of Roman history: the poet Quintus Horatius Flaccus is called

Horace, while Horatius was the name of several legendary heroes, among them "Horatius of the Bridge." Horatio was the name of the great English naval hero, Lord Nelson.

Howard From the Old German, meaning "watchman."

Hubert From the Old German, meaning "bright mind."

Hugh From the Anglo-Saxon, meaning "mind-thought."

Humphrey From the Teutonic, meaning "grant peace."

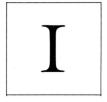

I

Ian The Scottish form of *John.*

Immanuel From the Hebrew, meaning "God is with us." A fine old biblical name, though little used in modern times. Variants include *Emanuel* and *Imanuel.*

Isaac From the Hebrew, meaning "laughter." In the Bible the son and the father of Abraham.

Ishmael From the Hebrew, meaning "God hearkens."

Jack See *Jacob* and *John.*

Jacob From the Hebrew, meaning "supplanter." Jacob's twelve sons were the fathers of the twelve tribes of Israel. In its national variants—among them the English *James*—one of the most enduring and popular male names.

James The English form of *Jacob.* A name popular with English royalty, also borne by five American Presidents (Madison, Monroe, Polk, Buchanan, and Garfield).

Jarrell See *Gerald.*

Jason From the Greek, meaning "healer." A name that has become extraordinarily popular, verging on the trendy.

Jedidiah From the Hebrew, meaning "God is my friend."

Jefferson A patronymic form of *Jeffrey* or *Geoffrey.*

Jeffrey See *Geoffrey.*

Jeremiah From the Hebrew, meaning "God has appointed."

Jeremy See *Jeremiah.*

Jesse From the Hebrew, meaning "the Lord is."

John From the Hebrew, meaning "God is gracious." Of all names, perhaps the most popular. Every area of human endeavor has been graced with a celebrated bearer of this name, from Milton, Donne, and Keats, to Locke, Dewey, and Audubon, to Adams, his son John Quincy Adams, and John Fitzger-

ald Kennedy. Its national variants are equally popular: *Evan* (Welsh), *Sean* (Irish), *Johann* (German), *Jean* (French), *Ian* (Scottish), and *Ivan* (Russian). Jack and Johnny are common nicknames.

Jonah From the Hebrew, meaning "dove." *Jonas* is a variant.

Jonathan From the Hebrew, meaning "God has given."

Joseph From the Hebrew, meaning "he shall add." A name from both the Old Testament (the son of Jacob and Rachel) and the New Testament (the husband of Mary) that has long been popular. Joe is the nickname.

Joshua From the Hebrew, meaning "God is my salvation." A biblical name widely bestowed in recent times.

Julian From the Latin, perhaps meaning "divine" or "soft-haired." Originally derived from the Latin *Julius*.

Justin From the Latin, meaning "just."

K·L

Karl See *Charles.*

Keith Origin uncertain. Perhaps from the Gaelic, meaning "the wind," and originally a surname or a variant of *Kenneth.*

Kenneth From the Celtic, meaning "handsome."

Kevin From the Gaelic, meaning "handsome."

Kirby From the Old English, meaning "church."

Kiril, Kyril See *Cyril.*

Laurence From the Latin, meaning "laurel." *Lawrence* is a variant spelling. Larry is the nickname.

Lemuel From the Hebrew, meaning "devoted to God." A name popular with our Puritan forefathers.

Leo From the Latin, meaning "lion." *Leon* is a variant form.

Leonard From the German, meaning "bold lion."

Lesley From the Old English, meaning "meadow"; probably originated as a place-name. *Leslie* is a variant spelling.

Lloyd From the Welsh, meaning "gray."

Louis From the Old High German, meaning "warrior prince." The name of the kings of France, most notably the Sun King, Louis XIV. Its Germanic form is *Ludwig,* also a royal name; *Lewis* is a variant spelling. The nickname *Lou* is less elegant.

M

Malcolm From the Celtic, meaning "disciple of Columbia" (sixth-century Scottish missionary).

Marcus From the Latin, although the meaning is uncertain; perhaps from Mars, the god of war. A favorite in the nineteenth century, Marcus—which has an appealingly formal sound—has given way to *Mark*.

Mark Origin uncertain; perhaps from the Latin, the god of war, Mars. The name of one of the four Evangelists and, for this and other reasons, perennially popular since the nineteenth century.

Marshal(1) Originally, and primarily, a surname.

Martin From the French via the Latin, meaning "of Mars," the god of war.

Mason From the French, meaning "stone worker."

Matthew From the Hebrew, meaning "gift of God." Matt is a popular nickname.

Maurice From the French, meaning "Moorish." *Morris* is the English variant form.

Maximilian From the Latin, meaning "great." A name said to have been coined by Frederic III of Germany for his son, Maximilian I, emperor of the Holy Roman Empire.

Michael From the Hebrew, meaning "who is like God." In the Bible the name of the archangel closest to God. A tremendously popular name in all of its national variants, which include *Michel, Mitchell, Mikhail, Michele,* and *Migele.* Mike is the nickname most commonly bestowed.

Miles Origin uncertain. An English form, perhaps from the Greek or a name derived from *Michael.* In America the first name of Puritan Miles Standish.

Mitchell A form of *Michael.*

Montague From the French, meaning "mountain." *Montgomery* is the English form of this elegant name.

Morgan From the Gaelic, meaning "sea-white," or the Welsh, meaning "great."

Morris A form of *Maurice.*

Nathaniel From the Hebrew, meaning "gift of God." An eminent name, borne by one of America's greatest writers, Nathaniel Hawthorne (1804–1864), author of *The Scarlet Letter*. Nat and Nate are nicknames.

Neal See *Neil*.

Nehemiah From the Hebrew, meaning "God is comfort." Popular in the Puritan era, perhaps because it is the name of one of the books of the Bible.

Neil From the Celtic, meaning "champion."

Nelson Originally a surname, meaning "son of Neil." The exploits of English Admiral Horatio Nelson (1758–1805) made this a popular name in England, as well as in the United States.

Nevil(le) From the French, meaning "new city."

Nicholas From the Greek, meaning "victory of the people." The name of the patron saint of Russia, after whom Czar Nicholas I was named. *Colin* is the English form; Nick is a pet name.

Nigel Origin uncertain. Perhaps from the Latin, meaning "dark." As a Scottish name, it occurs in the Domesday Book, the record of the survey of England made in 1086 by William the Conqueror.

Noah From the Hebrew, meaning "rest." Associated by most people with him of the Ark and Flood.

O-Q

Oliver From the Latin, meaning "olive tree."

Oscar From the Anglo-Saxon, meaning "divine spear."

Owen From the Welsh, meaning either "lamb" or "young."

Patrick From the Latin, meaning "of noble descent." Undoubtedly the most famous bearer of the name is the patron saint of Ireland.

Paul From the Latin, meaning "small." One of the twelve Apostles.

Percival From the French, meaning "pierce the valley." While *Percy* is more properly a nickname, it has frequently been bestowed as a first name, even among the aristocracy.

Peter From the Greek, meaning "rock." Since the time of the Apostles, when Simon was renamed Peter, this has been a consistently popular name throughout the world. Among its national variants are *Petrus* (Latin), *Piers* (English), *Pierre* (French), *Pietro* (Italian), and *Pedro* (Spanish and Portuguese).

Philip From the Greek, meaning "lover of horses." A noble name, borne by one of the Apostles and the father of Alexander the Great, among others. Phil is a nickname.

Quentin From the Latin, meaning "fifth."

Quincy A variant form of *Quentin*.

R

Ralph From the Anglo-Saxon, meaning "wolf-counsel." *Raoul* (French) and *Randolph* (English) are variant forms.

Ramsey From the Old English, originally a place-name meaning "wooded island."

Randal(1) See *Randolph.*

Randolph From the Anglo-Saxon, meaning "shield wolf."

Raymond From the Old French, meaning "wise protection."

Reginald From the Teutonic, meaning "judgment power."

Richard From the Old High German, meaning "strong ruler." A name with English royal antecedents, among them the daring Richard the Lion Hearted. Rich and Rick are two common pet forms of the name.

Robert From the Anglo-Saxon, meaning "bright fame." A consistently popular name that is much beloved in many of its national variants, including *Robin* and *Rupert* (English), *Robbie* (Scotch), and *Roberto* (Italian and Spanish). Robbie is also a nickname, as are Rob, Robby, Bob, and Bobby.

Robin See *Robert.*

Robinson A patronymic form of *Robin.* See *Robert.*

Roderic(k) From the Old German, meaning "famous ruler." *Rory* is the Irish form. Rod is the nickname.

Rodney Origin unknown. Perhaps a variant of *Roderick.*

Roland is valorous and Oliver is wise.
Song of Roland

Roger From the Old German, meaning "fame-spear."

Roland From the Old High German, meaning "famous land."
The name of the greatest of Charlemagne's warriors, celebrated
in Ariosto's *Orlando Furioso* and the medieval *Song of Roland*.

Rory See *Roderick*.

Ross Meaning unknown. Originally a surname in Scotland that
has become a first name.

Rudolph From the Old High German, meaning "famous wolf."

Rupert The German form of *Robert*. This name was imported
into England with Rupert, Prince of Palatine, nephew of
Charles I, and became a royalist favorite during the English
Civil War.

Russel(1) From the French, meaning "red."

S

Samuel From the Hebrew, meaning "his name is God." The name of the prophet who anointed Saul as the first king of Israel. Sam is sometimes given as a first name, although properly it is only a nickname.

Scot(t) From the English, meaning "a native of Scotland."

Sean The Irish form of *John*.

Sebastian From the Greek, meaning "venerable."

Seth From the Hebrew, meaning either "compensation" or "appointed." In the Bible Seth was the third child of Adam and Eve.

Seymour Origin uncertain. Probably a place-name either from the Old English or the French; in any case, certainly a surname of English nobility before it was a first name. (Jane Seymour was the third wife of Henry VIII.)

Sidney From the French (originally *Saint Denis*). *Sydney* is a variant spelling.

Simeon From the Hebrew, meaning "hearing." *Simon* is a variant form.

Stanley From the Old English, originally a place-name meaning "stony meadow."

Stephen From the Greek, meaning "crown." A beautiful and ever-popular name. *Steven* is a variant spelling, and Steve is a pet name.

T·V

Terence From the Latin, originally a Roman family name. Terry is a nickname for Terence, not a proper name.

Thad(d)eus From the Greek and Latin, meaning "gift of God." Thad is a pleasant nickname.

Theodore From the Greek, meaning "God's gift." Ted, Teddy, and Theo are nicknames.

Thomas From the Hebrew and Aramaic, meaning "twin." In the Bible one of the twelve Apostles; "doubting Thomas" was so called because he doubted Christ's resurrection. A prominent name, borne by many great men in all walks of life, including the philosopher Saint Thomas Aquinas, President Thomas Jefferson, and inventor Thomas Alva Edison. Alas, a disadvantage to the name is the nickname *Tommy* applied to men over fifteen years of age.

Timothy From the Greek, meaning "to honor God." In the Bible Timothy was the friend of Saint Paul. Tim is a nickname.

Tobiah From the Hebrew, meaning "God is good." Though Tobiah and its variant *Tobias* have an antique ring, both are fine names. Toby, however, is merely a pet name, as is the more unusual Tobin.

Tristram From the Celtic, meaning "a herald."

Victor From the Latin, meaning "conqueror." Undoubtedly because of its meaning, a name popular with Italian kings and popes, as well as many others of equally noble pursuits.

Vincent From the Latin, meaning "victor."

W·Z

Walter From the Teutonic, meaning "to rule." A name imported into England by the Normans after 1066.

Wendell Origin uncertain. Either from the Teutonic, meaning "wanderer," or from the Anglo-Saxon, "valley." A name afforded distinction by some of the men who bore it, including Oliver Wendell Holmes, Chief Justice of the Supreme Court, and politician Wendell Wilkie.

William From the Teutonic, meaning "helmet." A name popular with English kings from William the Conqueror (1066) to the present-day Prince William, and three American Presidents (William Henry Harrison, William McKinley, and William Taft). *Willis* is a variant form, and Bill(y) and Will(ie) are pet names.

Winthrop From the Anglo-Saxon, originally a place-name. Winthrop is also a surname; Win is a pet name.

Woodrow From the Anglo-Saxon, originally a place-name meaning "passage in the woods." The best known bearer of the name is American President Woodrow Wilson.

Zacharia, Zecharia From the Hebrew, meaning "God has remembered." A variant form is *Zachary*, an eminent name borne by the twelfth President of the United States, Zachary Taylor (1784–1858).

Zachary See *Zacharia*.

《我的第一本名人传记漫画书》系列，
在美国、韩国、中国大陆以及台湾等地出版以来，
受到广泛好评！

W9-CTT-527

畅销书《好妈妈胜过好老师》作者 尹建莉：这是一套培养孩子阅读兴趣的好书，也是一套保护孩子梦想和创造力的好书！

中国绕月探测二期工程"嫦娥二号"卫星总指挥 张廷新：人在整个太空中是非常渺小的个体，但是一个人的思想却可以是浩瀚无垠的，可以思考万物的起源，可以探索宇宙的奥秘！

中国绕月探测二期工程"嫦娥二号"卫星总设计师 黄江川：我小时候最渴望的就是这样一套书，可以近距离地接触自己的偶像，现在这个愿望终于在我儿子身上实现了。

中国台湾作家及节目主持人 吴淡如：奥普拉是成功的女企业家，她很有才华，影响社会，也回馈社会。与恶劣的环境搏斗，在不可能中创造可能，是最激励人心的故事。

中国台北市立图书馆馆长 洪世昌：她是成功的脱口秀主持人，幽默、机智又言之有物。言之有物基于她通过广泛阅读所积累的知识。希望小朋友阅读本书时，除了看到奥普拉的成功，也不忘记她背后的努力，从小培养阅读的习惯。

中国空间技术研究院科研人员 赵臻：爱迪生是所有孩子的典范。他让功课平平的孩子知道，只要肯尝试、不怕难，将来一样充满希望。他让有天分的孩子明白，天才也要有99%的努力，才能开创成功的未来。

中国台北艺术大学校长 朱宗庆：当一个小孩儿以无比的好奇心来实验，藉由"拆解"来"理解"这个世界，请给他掌声！

著名电影导演 周星驰：我看斯皮尔伯格的《E.T.》时还在电视训练班，直到现在我仍记得当时所受到的感动和震撼——原来科幻片可以拍成这样！可以这样说，正因为斯皮尔伯格，我才立志要当导演。

中国台北教育大学儿童英语教育研究所所长 张湘君：迪士尼肯定自己的想法且勇于实践，即使只是涂鸦，也能成就大事业。本书让孩子知道梦想与现实之间的距离是有办法拉近的。

中国台湾政治大学国际关系研究中心第一所主任 郑端耀：用生动的漫画呈现林肯的奋斗过程，寓教于乐，是亲子共读的好书。通过林肯的故事，让孩子知道在逆境中仍可实践理想，心怀感恩。

中国台湾辅仁大学历史系教授 张四德：希望小朋友学习林肯：敞开心怀，努力学习，提升自己的见识；敞开心怀，付出关怀，世界更美好！

看漫画，读故事，学语文，

 本书阅读指南

直观概括 一目了然

在讲述每个名人的成长故事之前，"名人大脚印"会告诉大家这个名人的基本概况，为的是让孩子们在读故事之前对这个名人有一个整体的概念，相当于跟这个名人初次见面。

深入思考 启发阅读

每章的开篇，都设有"阅读小脚印"，每个小脚印里都有几个问题，带着这些问题去阅读这一章的故事，可以让孩子更好地理解故事的主要内容。有了这些小脚印，家长们也可以参与到阅读中来，引导孩子阅读。

阅读小脚印

阅读小脚印
1. 苹果公司的创始人是谁？
2. 苹果的名字是怎么来的？
3. 第一台苹果是在哪里生产出来的？
4. 没有钱买零件，乔布斯想出了什么好办法？

孩子课外阅读的最佳选择！

他的小故事，我的大道理

苹果的两个史蒂夫——史蒂夫·乔布斯和史蒂夫·沃兹尼亚克一直被人们传为佳话。虽然都叫史蒂夫，他们两个性格却截然相反。乔布斯向来我行我素、个性张扬、激情澎湃，而沃兹则性格温和、憨厚可爱。但是对电子产品的热爱以及无限创意又让他们志同道合，并且充分达到了优势互补。沃兹能搞定复杂的电路设计，却因为不擅言辞很难给别人说明白。乔布斯则天生就有推销的本领，总能把沃兹的设计用最浅显的语言表述出来，并转变成生产力，变成真金白银。他俩携手创办了苹果公司，并且共同研发出第一台苹果电脑。没有沃兹的帮助，或许就不会有乔布斯今天的传奇。

朋友是人生中不可或缺的重要元素。找到和你志同道合的朋友，你会终身受益。

积累语文素材
学习名人品质

每章的结束都设有"他的小故事，我的大道理"，每个小故事都可以成为孩子们的写作素材，每个大道理都可以帮助孩子更好地学习名人优秀的品质。

解决问题
助力成长

每个人的成长过程中都会遇到大大小小的问题，我们该如何解决？这个环节旨在培养孩子解决实际问题的能力。这里列举了很多名人遇到的问题，通过他们遇到问题时的解决方式来引导孩子思考。

如果我是他，我会怎么办？

乔布斯和沃兹获得了成功，大家很开心。当众人都把目光聚焦在沃兹的技术上时，乔布斯的心理发生了微妙的变化。他觉得自己才是主角，自己才应该受到关注，因此产生了自己单干的想法，结果最后失败了。看到身边的好朋友取得成就，你会怎么办呢？

更多关于《我的第一本名人传记漫画书》（第一辑）的精彩互动请见《播撒欢乐的动画大师沃尔特·迪士尼》一书的互动园地。

如何让自己的梦想变为现实？《我的第一本名人传记漫画书》系列丛书会给大家提供答案。这些名人小时候并没有富裕的家境，也不具备超能力。他们就是和我们一样平凡的人，不，也许他们的成长环境比我们更加艰苦和恶劣。即便如此，他们也没有忘记为自己的未来酝酿"梦想"，并为之付出了坚持不懈的努力。真诚希望阅读这套系列丛书的小朋友们，都能拥有一个属于自己的"梦想"。

韩国小学社会课教育研究会

《我的第一本名人传记漫画书》系列丛书，一改过去一代所读过的那种冗长、教条的风格，采取了孩子们喜闻乐见的形式，容易让他们产生亲近感，更容易引发孩子学习和思考。因此，我向家长和孩子们积极推荐这套书。

韩国教育心理学专家 宋仁燮

您了解孩子的梦想吗？您是否与您的孩子谈起过他们的梦想？令人惋惜的是，现在的家长更注重孩子的学习成绩，而忽视孩子对未来的梦想。他们总是认为学习成绩不高，无论什么样的梦想都不可能得以实现。

看了这套书，您将意识到保护好孩子的梦想有多么重要。有了梦想，不需要强迫孩子努力，他就能带着激情去学习。《我的第一本名人传记漫画书》会成为父母家教的好帮手。

（株）非常教育学习研究所所长 朴在元

一套好书对孩子一生的影响不可估量。

中国台湾"教育部长" 吴清基

我的第一本名人传记漫画书

用苹果改变世界的IT领袖

史蒂夫·乔布斯

（韩）金元植 著　权赫律等 译
（韩）青飞工作室 绘

吉林出版集团有限责任公司

图书在版编目（CIP）数据

用苹果改变世界的IT领袖史蒂夫·乔布斯/（韩）金元植著；（韩）青飞工作室绘；权赫律等译. -- 长春：吉林出版集团有限责任公司, 2012.6

（我的第一本名人传记漫画书）书名原文: Who? Steve Jobs

ISBN 978-7-5463-9000-0

Ⅰ.①用… Ⅱ.①金… ②青… ③权… Ⅲ.①乔布斯，S.（1955～2011）—传记—通俗读物 Ⅳ.①K837.125.38-49

中国版本图书馆CIP数据核字（2012）第061436号

WHO? STEVE JOBS

Copyright © 2010 Dasan Books Co., Ltd.

All rights reserved.

Original Korean edition was published by Dasan Books Co., Ltd.

Simplified Chinese language edition © 2012 by Jilin Publishing Group Co.,Ltd.

Simplified Chinese edition is published by arrangement with Dasan Books Co., Ltd.

版权所有 不准翻印

用苹果改变世界的IT领袖史蒂夫·乔布斯

著　　者：（韩）金元植
绘　　者：（韩）青飞工作室
译　　者：权赫律　等
创意设计：范中华　陈　曲
发行筹划：耿　宏　孟祥北
项目负责人：陈　曲
责任编辑：陈　曲　金　昊
出　　版：吉林出版集团有限责任公司
发　　行：吉林出版集团社科图书有限公司
电　　话：0431-86012701
印　　刷：北京威远印刷厂
开　　本：570mm×1020mm　1/12
印　　张：14
版　　次：2012年6月第1版
印　　次：2015年6月第2次印刷
书　　号：ISBN 978-7-5463-9000-0
定　　价：28.00元

如发现印装质量问题，影响阅读，请与印刷厂联系调换。

名人大脚印

嘿！大家好，我就是那个在车库中创立了苹果电脑的史蒂夫·乔布斯。你们用的iMac、iPod、iPad、iPhone手机都是我的杰作，这些艺术品让无数潮人为之疯狂，彻夜排队购买。我让苹果电脑的股价从每股17美元翻了几十倍，总市值突破5000个亿，比很多国家的总财富还多。我的皮克斯公司还制作出《玩具总动员》《海底总动员》《怪物公司》等好看的动画电影。我常说，活着就是为了改变世界，难道还有别的什么理由吗？

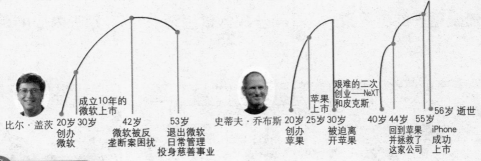

比尔·盖茨
20岁 30岁 成立10年的
微软上市
创办
微软
42岁
微软被反
垄断案困扰
53岁
退出微软
日常管理
投身慈善事业

史蒂夫·乔布斯
20岁 25岁 30岁
创办
苹果
苹果
上市
被迫离
开苹果
艰难的二次
创业——NeXT
和皮克斯
40岁 44岁 55岁
回到苹果
并拯救了
这家公司
iPhone
成功
上市
56岁 逝世

我的人生曲线

看完我和比尔·盖茨人生曲线的对比，你会发现，我的经历曲折得多，更容易让人联想到"传奇"，只不过只有我知道，过程是多么不容易。

我的狂言狂语

年轻时，我对沃兹讲过，有朝一日我会成为人类的引路人；成名之后，我对记者说自己的梦想是"在宇宙中留下一点印迹"；在2007年发布iPhone时，我说我想重新发明电话……如今，凭着我的激情与梦想，我真的做到了！

我让科技变得很酷

我带领苹果推出了iMac、iPod、iPad、iPhone手机等产品，我的想法很简单，就是让科技变得简单，让科技引领潮流，让苹果成为潮人的必备品。只要一根手指轻轻一点，就能玩转科技。

我的完美主义

我崇尚简约而不简单，我可以一辈子只穿T恤衫、牛仔裤和运动鞋，但是我的产品一定要简单、精致、完美，不仅仅是电子产品，还要是件艺术品。

目录

第一章

热爱电子的小男孩

1955年，在美国加州旧金山的一所医院里，一个年轻的未婚妈妈生下了一个小男孩儿。她没有能力独自抚养孩子长大，就委托社会福利机构为孩子寻找适合的养父母。

女士，请您在这里签字。

哦……

…

孩子交给我们，您就放心吧，我们一定会帮他找个好家庭的。

唉，好吧。

我能再抱抱他吗？

当然，轻点儿。

孩子，原谅妈妈吧，妈妈实在没有办法，才把你送人。

我的孩子呀……呜……

啊……
啊……

经过福利机构的严格挑选以及婴儿母亲的同意，这个小婴儿最后被保罗和克拉拉·乔布斯这对夫妇收养，他们给他取名叫史蒂夫·保罗·乔布斯。

亲爱的，快来看呀，史蒂夫会笑啦！

哈哈，太棒了，你看，他好像认得你。

亲爱的，他是上帝赐给我们的最棒的礼物，我们一定要尽全力把他抚养成人。

没错，我们会是这世界上最棒的父母。

史蒂夫，只要你健康成长，我们就心满意足了。为了你，我们愿意付出一切。

乔布斯在学校常常搞恶作剧，成了无法适应学校环境的问题孩子。

在乔布斯读四年级时，他的班里换了一位新老师。

史蒂夫？

叫我？

对，是我，没错。我就是那个万人烦的史蒂夫。

哦？是吗？

哇，你一定就是那个大名鼎鼎的史蒂夫。

他完全变了。

真的变了!

在希尔老师耐心的帮助下,乔布斯对学校的课程越来越感兴趣,他开始爱上学习。乔布斯成功后,常常说希尔老师是他生命中的贵人。

一年以后,在学校。

希尔老师,您找我们……史蒂夫又惹麻烦了吗?

嗯,史蒂夫……

老师,真对不起,他一直都是个淘气的孩子,我们会对他严加管教的。

哈哈,今天我请你们来,不是说这个。

他的小故事，我的大道理

　　乔布斯从小就对电子元器件表现出浓厚的兴趣。他常常把家里的电器偷偷地拆掉，然后再摸索着一点一点地装回去。家里的收音机、电视机等无一幸免，都在他手中"翻新"过。乔布斯全家搬到加利福尼亚州的洛斯阿尔托斯市后，史蒂夫觉得自己进了天堂：他总能在各处的箱子里翻到一两只废弃不用的电子元件，拆开来看个究竟，玩上好几个小时。正是由于他对电子学的无限热爱，才使得他后来与电脑结缘，成为了改变世界的人。

　　兴趣是最好的老师。所有的热情、勇气以及不断探索的动力，往往都源于浓厚的兴趣。如果你对某方面特别感兴趣，那就继续深入探索吧，说不定你就是下一个改变世界的人。

如果我是他，我会怎么办？

　　当乔布斯向老师说出了自己的真实想法后，不但没有得到老师的理解，反而遭到了批评。这使乔布斯产生了逆反心理，一气之下顶撞了老师，冲出教室。在学校里，遇到老师或者同学和自己想法不一致，得不到大家的理解的时候怎么办？是消极反抗，还是智慧化解？

如果我是他……

_____

_____

第一次尝试经营

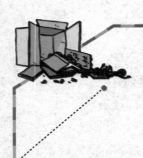

阅读小脚印

1. 中学时，乔布斯和谁成了最好的朋友？
2. 乔布斯无意中听到了什么事情，让他感到困惑？
3. 中学时的乔布斯显现出了什么才能？
4. 乔布斯第一次尝试做生意，结果怎么样？

房屋租金上涨，为了节省家庭开支，乔布斯一家搬到了郊区，乔布斯进入了当地的一所中学就读。

在这里，学校的教育理念和教学设施都很落后，乔布斯很不适应新的校园生活。为了乔布斯的将来，他的父母决定再次搬家。

哇，爸爸，你看那边成堆的电子零件！是半导体吗？

我听说住在这里的人好多都是工程师，在惠普那样的大公司工作。

爸爸，您说惠普？

乔布斯回想起自己10岁去惠普公司参观的情形。

同学们，摆在我们面前的是一台电脑，它能通过程序自动处理数据。

哇，自动啊！

不好意思，可以让我过去看一下吗？

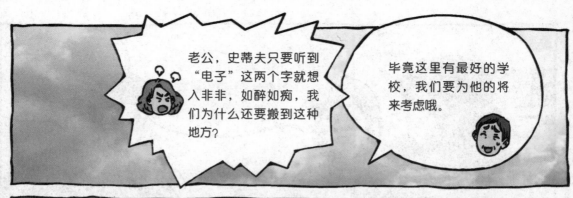

老公，史蒂夫只要听到"电子"这两个字就想入非非，如醉如痴，我们为什么还要搬到这种地方？

毕竟这里有最好的学校，我们要为他的将来考虑哦。

上了高中后，乔布斯加入了电子社团，他对电子的浓厚兴趣只增不减。一天，他在朋友的介绍下，结识了一位电脑奇才——史蒂夫·沃兹尼亚克。

那是你们做的吗？

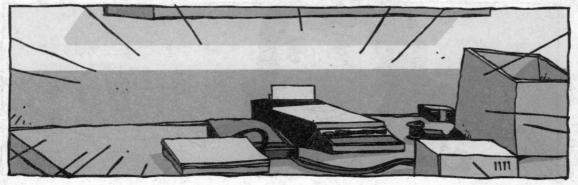

乔布斯和沃兹尼亚克一拍即合，常一起在乔布斯家的车库中忙活到深夜。两个人的友谊更加牢固了。

史蒂夫长大了。

是呀，我印象中他还是个小婴儿，现在他已经是高中二年级的学生了。

真的很感谢老天让我们拥有一个这么健康、聪明的儿子。

我不是爸妈亲生的孩子？老天，你别和我开这种玩笑！

我的亲生父母为什么要抛弃我？

乔布斯无意中得知自己是被领养的孩子。

天呀，我真不愿意相信，这是真的……

乔布斯知道了自己的身世后，一度陷入迷茫，开始变得叛逆，并成为了"嬉皮士"。（指西方国家中具有颓废派作风的人，他们由于对现实不满而采取玩世不恭的态度，如留长发、穿奇装异服等。）

嘿，史蒂夫！有阵子不见了，想我没？

沃兹！在这里看到你可真开心！

怎么样？你最近在忙什么？有什么新鲜事吗？

当然有！

你听说过没有？最近流行一种可以免费打电话的新方法，就是用一种哨音去干扰电话公司的电脑系统。

沃兹尼亚克成功做出能打免费恶搞电话的"小蓝盒",这款蓝色盒子只要按一个按钮就能拨打免费电话,比其他恶搞免费电话的装置更好用。

沃兹尼亚克的"小蓝盒"引起很多恶搞免费电话者的注意,乔布斯和沃兹尼亚克很快就在恶搞免费电话的圈子里出了名。

史蒂夫,你说什么?你想要卖"小蓝盒"?

是呀,我们大量采购零件然后制作,就能把成本控制在40元以内,然后再以150元左右的价格卖出去,并承诺我们会提供免费维修服务,你觉得怎么样?

听起来不错。

你仔细算算，只要能卖出去，绝对能赚钱！是个不错的生意。

生意？

以前真没发现，史蒂夫还有这样的商业头脑。这是天赋吗？

你就专心做产品吧，我去销售。相信我，没错的。

照你算的利润，应该问题不大，那就试试吧。

嘿嘿，这才是我喜欢的沃兹！放心吧，我去搞定原材料！

正如乔布斯预料的，"小蓝盒"很畅销，甚至供不应求。他们的生意做得红红火火。

你们是来买"小蓝盒"的吗？

是呀，听说那个可以很方便地拨打免费电话？

哈哈，就是这个。你看看，消息传得还真快哦！

这就是大名鼎鼎的"小蓝盒"呀！看你岁数不大，这个是你自己做的吗？

不是，我只是负责销售，这是我的好朋友做的。如果出故障了我们负责免费维修，你们可以随时联系我。

用苹果改变世界的IT领袖史蒂夫·乔布斯

他的小故事，我的大道理

苹果的两个史蒂夫——史蒂夫·乔布斯和史蒂夫·沃兹尼亚克一直被人们传为佳话。虽然都叫史蒂夫，他们两个性格却截然相反。乔布斯向来我行我素、个性张扬、激情澎湃，而沃兹则性格温和、憨厚可爱。但是对电子产品的热爱以及无限创意又让他们志同道合，并且充分达到了优势互补。沃兹能搞定复杂的电路设计，却因为不擅言辞很难给别人说明白。乔布斯则天生就有推销的本领，总能把沃兹的设计用最浅显的语言表述出来，并转变成生产力，变成真金白银。他俩携手创办了苹果公司，并且共同研发出第一台苹果电脑。没有沃兹的帮助，或许就不会有乔布斯今天的传奇。

朋友是人生中不可或缺的重要元素。找到和你志同道合的朋友，你会终身受益。

如果我是他，我会怎么办？

乔布斯和沃兹因为研发并兜售"小蓝盒"被警察逮捕了，还差点儿因此坐牢。他们的第一笔生意就这样泡汤了，可是沃兹和乔布斯在回家的路上就重新振作起来，开始计划下一次合作。很多人受挫以后就会变得小心翼翼，甚至就此放弃。如果你遇到了挫折，你会怎么办呢？

如果我是他……

第三章

倾听内心的声音

阅读小脚印

1. 大学时乔布斯对什么方面的课程产生了兴趣？
2. 乔布斯的第一份工作是如何争取到的？
3. 乔布斯为什么要去印度？
4. 乔布斯的印度之行让他领悟到了什么？

高中毕业后，乔布斯选择了俄勒冈州波特兰市的里德学院读大学。在这里，乔布斯结识了他的新朋友丹尼尔·科特克，两人都对佛教禅宗痴迷，成了亲密伙伴。

史蒂夫，你又逃课了？

科特克！

你最近在忙什么？

科特克，我决定要离开了。

我要休学！大学里没有我想学的东西，我不想再留在这里浪费时间、浪费金钱了，我宁愿回家做点儿我喜欢的事。

什么？

史蒂夫，不再考虑一下吗？我真舍不得你。

傻瓜，我会和你保持联系的，你是我大学里最要好的朋友。

不过，如果哪天我突然给你打电话，你可别惊讶哦。

嘿嘿！

大学生活一直没能吸引乔布斯。对大学生活感到厌倦的乔布斯，最终选择离开，他休学了。

乔布斯的工作都很琐碎乏味，和他最初的想象一点儿都不一样。

乔布斯的热情渐渐消退，他开始思考自己到底应该做什么。

喂，科特克，我是史蒂夫，你还好吗？

还凑合，你走了以后，生活少了很多乐趣，挺无聊的。你呢？

我也是，无聊极了！你想不想跟我一起去印度？

在印度，看到众多靠乞讨生活的人，乔布斯受到极大的震撼。他原以为只有懒惰的人才会贫穷，但很快他就发现，贫穷是印度平民无法逃脱的命运。

这里和我想象中的完全不同，之前我的想法真是太幼稚了。

啊！

老人家，我们可不可以跟您换一下衣服穿呢？

？

史蒂夫！你疯了吗？

你觉得有必要这样做吗？我全身都要痒死啦！

咱们总不能穿着牛仔裤当苦行僧吧？这样穿不是挺凉快的吗？习惯就好了。

<注>巴巴：印度民众对苦行僧的称呼。

啊？你是印度巴巴（注）？

他在说什么？

好像是让我们跟着他去。

这是要把我们带到哪里呀？

在巴巴高僧的带领下，乔布斯和科特克也参加了村里的盛会。巴巴还亲自为乔布斯落发。

史蒂夫，现在你也见到高僧了，有什么觉悟吗？

没有。说实话，我也没搞懂，为什么巴巴不理会其他来找他的人，就单独对我这么友好，为我落发了呢？

天晓得！老实说，我根本就不懂我们为什么要来这鬼地方。

啊？

啊，你说得对，科特克！

他的小故事，我的大道理

　　亲生父母对乔布斯的遗弃一直是他心中解不开的死结。寻找亲生父母失败后，他的精神一直处于极度迷茫的状态，他干脆休学，后来又跑到印度去，光着脚、穿着破烂衣服开始精神之旅。他穿上了僧侣的长袍，剃掉头发，开始吃素，并经常一个人静坐冥想，领悟禅宗。他越发冷漠，沉默寡言，但他内心的那种欲望仍旧没有得到满足。后来，他发现自己最热爱的还是电脑事业，并对此充满无限激情。他决定大干一场，遵从自己心底里的声音："改变世界！"

　　每个人都有迷茫或者叛逆的时候，但是请安静下来听一听，自己心底里的那个声音在讲什么。我们的时间有限，不要浪费时间为别人而活，不要因为其他人的观点而掩盖了自己内心的声音。

如果我是他，我会怎么办？

　　乔布斯休学后去电脑游戏公司毛遂自荐，可是却遭到了拒绝，并被批评是个不懂规矩、不可理喻的家伙。遭到别人拒绝的滋味很不好受，更何况被人批评甚至严厉斥责？可是乔布斯却非常执著，决不放弃。在遭到拒绝后，你还有勇气继续坚持吗？

如果我是他……

第四章

车库中诞生的苹果

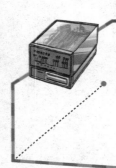

阅读小脚印

1. 苹果公司的创始人是谁？
2. 苹果的名字是怎么来的？
3. 第一台苹果是在哪里生产出来的？
4. 没有钱买零件，乔布斯想出了什么好办法？

从印度回来，乔布斯决定好好干一番事业。

沃兹，《大众电子》杂志你读过吗？有人发明了世界上第一台微型个人电脑。

嗯，我知道，名字叫"牛郎星"嘛！

朋友，你知道这意义有多么巨大吗？

现在，只有专家才能接触到电脑。不过，我想很快，每个家庭就都能拥有这种微型电脑了。

是的，它还可以和彩色屏幕连接起来工作，到时候，你可以用电视机当显示器。

太厉害了，我就知道你能行！

我感觉这台电脑在市场上会很有竞争力，你说，我们把它批量生产推向市场，怎么样？

啊？我还没想过要辞掉惠普公司的工作，组装电脑只是我自己的一点儿小爱好而已。

沃兹，这种能让你成为百万富翁的天赋，你难道想白白浪费掉？

想想，如果每个人的家里都摆放着你研制的电脑，那多酷啊！

嗯，但我对经营一点儿都不感兴趣。

哈哈，不敢当，过奖了。

如果名字一听就让人想到复杂的电脑元件，那太糟糕了，一点儿都不吸引人。

没错！"苹果电脑"听起来很有趣，又充满活力。

当然！我在想你是怎么想到的呢？

我们周围都是苹果园，那香味儿……所以，你懂的。

原来如此。

1976年4月1日，乔布斯和沃兹尼亚克成立了苹果电脑公司。尽管两个人都掏出了家底儿，并四处筹款，公司的原始注册资金也只有1000美元。

我相信你！咱们就努力做吧！

虽然我们没有自己的果园，但将来我们会制造出很多苹果。我绝对相信，这些苹果会令世人刮目相看的。

啊，等等，50台成品？

制造50台电脑，需要很多零部件，可我们根本没有那么多钱来买这些零件。

是啊，我怎么没想到？

你接订单的时候难道没有考虑过吗？搞砸了要付违约金的，我们就会负债累累！

别急，我会想办法弄到零件的。

这可不是容易的事。

别担心，无非是多花几天时间而已。

什么？

放心吧，我会找到需要的零件的，你就准备开工吧！

真是什么也难不倒你，史蒂夫。

乔布斯先生，恕我直言，你真是一个固执己见、不屈不挠的怪人。

......

好吧，我答应赊给你零部件。

真的？谢谢，多谢您，先生！

不过，我会先问一下Byte Shop电脑店的保罗，这份合约是否有效。明天给你回复。

什么？

先生，我今天就想要零部件，请您现在就去确认吧。

简直不可理喻！

乔布斯锲而不舍的精神最终打动了零部件供应商，供应商同意他赊账购买所需的全部零部件。

沃兹，现在我们可以开工了吧？

了不起，史蒂夫。

现在我们就是不吃不睡，也得在交货期限之前把电脑装出来！

没问题，交给我吧！

乔布斯和沃兹尼亚克夜以继日地赶制出了苹果的第一批产品。

很高兴为您送上我们的苹果电脑！您就等着大卖吧！

史蒂夫，我订的不是这种电脑。

什么？

我想要的是完全组装好的电脑，不是半成品。我订的电脑要有外壳、电源、键盘、显示器等全套设备。

不会吧？

我想我们对"组装"概念的理解有点偏差，我以为您要的是像"牛郎星"那样的装配组件。

噢！上帝！

史蒂夫，那我们送来的这些货怎么办？

我想尽量按照使用者的需求改进电脑的功能。

这个主意不错，既能让购买者满意，也会给经销商们带来惊喜。

嗯，我想让人机真正互动起来，利用键盘就可以输入信息。

好，如果是家用电脑的话，还得想办法降低噪音。

这一次，我们一定能一炮走红！让人们震惊！

哈哈！

1976年9月，乔布斯和沃兹尼亚克把他们的新电脑带到了亚特兰大市的电脑展会，他俩对这项新产品充满了信心。

个人电脑产业的发展速度，出乎乔布斯和沃兹尼亚克的预料，其他参展电脑拥有闪亮的金属外壳和键盘，抢尽了苹果的风头。

唉！在这么大的展馆里，我们的小公司显得太渺小了！

是啊，不过至少我们知道了自己与别人的差距，电脑行业发展得太迅速了。

人们想要操作起来更简单的电脑，就像电视，只要打开开关就能使用。电脑未来的需求者不是专家或专业人士，而是普通的家庭。

乔布斯联系了当地最有名的广告公司——雷吉斯·麦肯纳广告公司。

先生，您经常打电话来，不如我们见面谈吧。

你说的是苹果电脑？你们是在车库里研制出来的？

是的，我们在车库起家，却有最顶尖的技术，我们会制造出让美国，不，是让全世界为之赞叹的电脑。

我觉得他有些言过其实。

我知道，我们也有不足的地方。

哦？哪个方面？

我们应该与你们这样专业的人士开展合作！

尽管这次会面麦肯纳是想回绝固执的乔布斯，但最终却被他的热情和执著感染，答应了为苹果电脑做广告。

真是没有什么可以阻挡你前进，你的热情和执著令人敬佩！合作愉快！

与麦肯纳签约后，乔布斯有机会见到更多的投资者。在新投资者的支持下，乔布斯在1977年成立了苹果电脑有限公司。

你看，我说我们能行吧？现在我们就用苹果电脑让全世界惊叹吧！

听起来不错，我准备好了。

乔布斯和沃兹尼亚克加快速度，开发出他们的第二代个人电脑——Apple II。

apple

更重要的是，直到今天，只有电脑专家才会用电脑；但Apple II不一样，只要打开电源，每个人都会使用。

你的意思是，不需要输入复杂的程序语言？

是呀，听说是一套全新的操作系统，很亲切！

没有噪音。

真的听不到。

此外，Apple II 最大程度降低噪音，这样你的电脑听起来不会像一辆发动的赛车。

Apple II 的目标，是让在家里操作电脑成为一种人人喜爱的轻松的生活方式。

Apple II 让操作更简单，从此，电脑不再是专家和实验室独有，而是走进每个家庭。

他的小故事，我的大道理

　　乔布斯对事业充满激情，从不轻言放弃。亚特兰大市的电脑展会让乔布斯意识到：要想让科技创新转化为钞票，必须寻找投资方和广告宣传专业人士的帮助。从那时起，许多硅谷公司的老板就开始被一个长头发、胡子拉碴、穿着破洞牛仔裤的年轻人骚扰，每天都接到他打来的N次电话或者干脆被堵在办公室里。一开始乔布斯得到的是婉拒，后来干脆被严词拒绝，可这丝毫不影响乔布斯的热情。这个年轻人不停地推销着自己的梦想，热情洋溢地描绘着个人电脑的美好未来。最终他的热情感染了投资者，他获得了新的投资，并与广告创意公司签订合作协议。

　　请相信，你的热情可以感染其他人，你的态度最终决定了成败！

如果我是他，我会怎么办？

　　当苹果接到第一份订单后，却发现没有钱来买零部件，当时沃兹想到的是那会让自己背上很多债务，而乔布斯第一个想法就是"无非是多花几天时间而已"。乐观积极的人时刻都会为达成目标努力想办法，而心态保守的人就会先想到失败的后果，你是哪一种心态呢？

如果我是他……

25岁的亿万富翁

阅读小脚印

1. 乔布斯是什么时候进入富豪榜的？
2. 用鼠标来操作电脑，是谁先想到的？
3. 乔布斯主导开发的产品经历过哪些失败？
4. 苹果新产品的失败给乔布斯带来哪些影响？

Apple II 的问世，推动了个人电脑的发展进程。由于功能强大，操作越来越简单，电脑被越来越多的人所关注，电脑的需求量迅速增长。

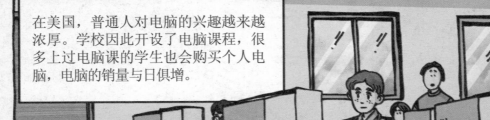

在美国，普通人对电脑的兴趣越来越浓厚。学校因此开设了电脑课程，很多上过电脑课的学生也会购买个人电脑，电脑的销量与日俱增。

到了1980年，苹果公司为了满足市场需求，已经发展成拥有一千多名员工的企业，并在海外开设分厂。

苹果的股票上市第一天，就取得了惊人的成绩，一小时不到就卖出了460万股，乔布斯一下子变成了世界上最年轻的亿万富翁，进入了富豪榜名单。

TIME
STRIKING IT RICH
America's Risk Takers

仅仅25岁的乔布斯，已经成为电脑行业的领军人物，在行业内备受瞩目。

请问，您就是史蒂夫·乔布斯先生吗？

哦，是我。

《时代》杂志封面有您的照片，您本人和照片一样帅气。

哈哈，您过奖了。

您就是Apple Ⅱ的设计者沃兹尼亚克先生?

嗯……我就是。

Apple Ⅱ可不是我自己独立完成的,是我和史蒂夫共同的杰作……

沃兹是天才,他的专业技术无人能敌。

在专业技术之上,我们又增加了很多新的时尚元素,例如外形简洁漂亮……

嗯,不是,我是……

佩服佩服,沃兹,您就是苹果科技创新的源头啦!

您太谦虚了,我听说您享有"硅谷天才工程师"的美誉。

不,真没什么。

我也曾当过工程师,我太理解了,像您这样优秀的科技人才,却并没有得到应有的重视。

乔布斯想用丽莎证明自己，这是他的野心；他想制造出世界上最好的电脑，这是他的热情。

我们会全力以赴！

正当乔布斯为开发丽莎忙得热火朝天的时候，传来一个坏消息。

老板，有件事……

沃兹尼亚克坠机了，因为头部受损，得了阶段性记忆缺失症。

事隔一天，苹果对比自己规模大10倍的IBM公司宣战，在一份很大的报刊上登了整页的广告来欢迎IBM进入个人电脑领域。

郑重欢迎IBM加入竞争

很期待IBM推出第一台个人电脑，从此进入个人电脑领域发展。苹果公司期待电脑行业的良性竞争，只有竞争才能推动行业的发展。我们感谢IBM对于研发个人电脑的慷慨投入与付出，并希望与IBM携手，将美国的这项科技推广至全球。

……

苹果公司

大家都辛苦了，经过测评，丽莎的设计和性能超过了市面上所有的个人电脑。

用鼠标的感觉真是太棒了，我相信鼠标很快就会成为所有电脑的标准配置。

那当然。

不过，成本方面完全超出了我们的预算，电脑价格要在一万美元以上，这是个大问题。

还有，丽莎的整体重量达到21千克，对于个人电脑来说，太笨重了。

为了达到最佳性能，这些是必须作出的牺牲。我想，消费者都是聪明人，他们会爱上丽莎的，丽莎值得他们拥有！

希望如此。

然而事与愿违，丽莎的市场反应不佳，只能卖给航天局等个别公司。而令乔布斯不屑的IBM个人电脑由于兼容性高，价格便宜，深受消费者欢迎。

我挑选了最顶尖的科技人才，研制出世上最棒的电脑，结果为什么会这样？

嗯，看来为了挽回败局，只有降价了。

丽莎怎么会被IBM打败？除了价格昂贵点儿，我真想不出其他原因。

乔布斯认为丽莎失败是由于价格太高，于是，他开始研发功能一样优秀、低价位的电脑麦金塔（Macintosh）。

决心挽回败局的乔布斯想到了广告投入，要在宣传上下工夫。

怎样才可以让我们最新推出的电脑麦金塔震惊世界？什么方式最有效呢？

乔布斯决定在美式足球超级杯中投放麦金塔电脑的广告，那是当时美国收视率最高的电视节目。广告中把麦金塔电脑描绘成救世主，把堕落到IBM手中的世人拯救出来。

广告仅仅播放了一次，就产生了巨大的反响，很多人都开始期待麦金塔电脑。

斯卡利，你觉得怎么样？

苹果公司经历了一连串的挫败后，挖来了曾经在百事可乐公司任职的约翰·斯卡利接任苹果的CEO。

广告做得很棒，令人印象深刻。

是啊，因为这个广告，人们都在谈论麦金塔电脑。

我的直觉告诉我，消费者想要的是跟烤面包机一样容易操作的电脑，麦金塔就是。所以，今年我们能轻松达到销售75万台的目标，我有信心。

嗯，看来你早已胸有成竹。我们前期已经投入了巨额资金，决不能让麦金塔电脑失败。

说得对！

1984年1月24日，麦金塔电脑在全国的店面销售。很多看过广告的民众聚集在店里，想要一睹新电脑的庐山真面目。

可是，看过了麦金塔电脑的消费者们立即改变了主意，转而去购买IBM的电脑，苹果再度成为IBM的手下败将。

屏幕也太小了，还是黑白的，看着不爽。

怎么内存就这么一点儿？自带软件也很少，光漂亮有什么用啊？

是呀，还比IBM贵！

最近苹果是被虫子咬了吗？推出的新品一点儿都不给力！

乔布斯在董事会空前孤立，面对大家的指责有口难辩，最终只好无奈地离开了苹果公司。

太无情了！他们怎么可以这样对我？

我居然被自己创办的公司解雇，这简直是耻辱。

他的小故事，我的大道理

刚刚过完30岁生日的乔布斯，被董事会赶出了苹果公司。当时，全美各大报纸上铺天盖地的都是他被罢黜的新闻。他的朋友默里担心他做傻事，赶往他的住处。在漆黑的房间里，乔布斯一个人孤独地躺在角落，默里过去紧紧地抱住他，两个人抱头痛哭起来。乔布斯这样描述过他对苹果的感情："如果苹果公司需要我扫地，我可以去扫地；需要我去扫厕所，我也可以清理厕所。我的心会一直在那里，我也会一直想念我的苹果。" 几天后，乔布斯重新振作起来，卖出了苹果公司的85万股股票，断了自己回苹果的退路。日后乔布斯感慨：如果没有这段经历，或许也不会有我的今天。

失败是成功之母。每个人都不愿意失败，但如果失败了，就要勇于面对，去开始下一次的尝试，找到通往成功的路。

如果我是他，我会怎么办？

乔布斯和沃兹获得了成功，大家很开心。当众人都把目光聚焦在沃兹的技术上时，乔布斯的心理发生了微妙的变化。他觉得自己才是主角，自己才应该受到关注，因此产生了自己单干的想法，结果最后失败了。看到身边的好朋友取得成就，你会怎么办呢？

如果我是他……

迎接新的挑战

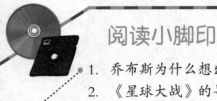

1. 乔布斯为什么想出用光盘代替软盘？
2. 《星球大战》的导演为什么会去找乔布斯？
3. 皮克斯制作的《玩具总动员》是哪一年在美国上映的？票房如何？

卸任之后，乔布斯的办公室被搬到苹果公司对面的一栋小楼里。

苹果公司给了乔布斯一个新职位：产品发起人，而这不过是个虚名，实际上他已经被迫退出公司管理层。

产品发起人

你可以选择继续留在苹果公司，但从现在起，你不再拥有任何职务与权利。

我辛苦多年创办了苹果公司，到头来我却成了局外人！

莫非我真的要离开？

乔布斯在苹果公司里成为了多余的人，面对这样残酷的事实，他感到无比伤心，甚至很绝望。

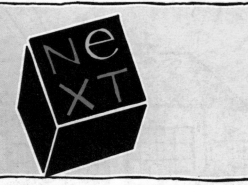

乔布斯深信他是最了解电脑的人，他最拿手的就是开发新电脑，于是他创立了他的第二家电脑公司NeXT。

欢迎你们从苹果公司出来跟我一起创业。

NeXT里的e代表的是"教育"，这将是我们公司的产品理念。

我计划生产专业领域的电脑，专为在实验室、大学和研究机构里工作的专业人士打造高性能的电脑。

这个电脑是什么样子的呢？

看我手里这个方盒子，这是光驱，我们的电脑将用光盘储存资讯。

光盘以光信息作为存储信息的载体，与当时的标准储存方式——软盘相比，光盘容量大，能够储存更多的资讯。

电脑软盘

电脑光盘

但是电脑装上光驱，成本就会变得更高。我怕……

使用者还必须买光盘，是不是构成了额外花销？

这个我想过了，NeXT电脑的使用者都是收入稳定的专业人士。

我坚信NeXT Cube电脑将会赢得消费者的青睐。

乔布斯夜以继日地研发新电脑，把全部期望寄托在NeXT Cube电脑上。终于，到了产品发布的那一天。

乔布斯先生，离开苹果5年后，你带着NeXT Cube电脑重返市场，这是你对苹果的反击吗？

哈哈，我的创新并非针对苹果，我有更远大的目标，就是制造出能为全世界作出贡献的电脑。

NeXT Cube设计得很漂亮，请介绍一下它的性能。

目前市场上主流的电脑售价大约是1500美元，NeXT Cube 6500美元的售价太贵了。

NeXT Cube电脑比麦金塔电脑更简单易用，它是目前世界上最容易操作、最快速、也是性能最高的电脑。

NeXT Cube电脑的失败让乔布斯的财务状况每况愈下。

唉！还有这么多库存。

是啊，和我们的销售预期相差太远了。

投进去的资金都变成了库存，怎么办？时间拖得越久，情况会越糟糕。

一天，乔布斯接到了《星球大战》导演乔治·卢卡斯的电话，请乔布斯去他的公司参观。

幸会，请问找我过来有什么事吗？

乔布斯先生，很高兴认识您。

这是我的电脑动画设计公司，我想您可能会感兴趣，因此决定请您来参观一下。

有了！我可以让他们发挥长处，为NeXT绘制软件，这样还可以促进NeXT Cube电脑的销量。

同时，我们再把这项服务卖给那些需要动画的人，像广告、宣传策划公司，赚他们的钱。

想明白了盈利模式的乔布斯信心满满，他自掏腰包投资了一千万美金，收购了乔治·卢卡斯的电脑动画设计公司。

1986年，皮克斯动画公司（Pixar）成立了，这里聚集了一群创意非凡的天才，他们富有想象力，有想法，充满热情。皮克斯的成立为乔布斯的东山再起拉开了序幕。

真是让人头疼，NeXT的电脑库存量还是很大。

你是说皮克斯也在赔钱？

是呀，皮克斯一直在亏损，已经亏损一千万美元了。

我看过，大部分亏损是因为3D立体动画的投入，这个部门目前还没法盈利。

嗯，但你看过他们制作的动画吗？好有趣呀！

什么？

现在一点儿钱都没赚到，你还笑得出来？再这样下去，我看你离破产不远了。

破产？

是该好好想想了。

可我不能撤掉投资，我不想看到他们失望的表情。皮克斯是个有创造力的团队，我相信他们的实力。

就按照计划继续投资吧。

什么？

他们有了钱才能制作出最棒的动画，还有时间。

可是……

乔布斯对皮克斯的前景充满信心，他非常信任他的团队，继续投入大量资金确保员工们能尽量发挥潜能。等到1989年，他漫长的等待终于开花结果。

《小锡兵》赢得了奥斯卡最佳动画短片奖，皮克斯获得了全世界的肯定。

第61届奥斯卡最佳动画短片奖的得主是……

皮克斯的《小锡兵》！

PIXAR
TINY TOY STORIES

第六章 迎接新的挑战 125

这是皮克斯全体员工共同努力的结果!

他们终于成功了!

皮克斯应该有更大的潜力,不应该局限在制作电脑软件动画上。

这些天才会创作出最优秀的动画,应该让他们在动画领域大显身手了!

1992年,皮克斯的发展机会来了。

世界上最大的动画公司——迪士尼对皮克斯设计的动画产生了兴趣。

WALT DISNEY

PICTURES

乔布斯先生,皮克斯高超的动画水平太令人敬佩了。

谢谢,他们确实很棒。

这时，NeXT公司的经营陷入困境，乔布斯不得不把所有赌注都压在皮克斯的第一部动画长片《玩具总动员》上面。

动画制作的过程中，出现了很多难题，可皮克斯团队的每个人都热情高涨，他们把所有精力投入到《玩具总动员》的创作中，终于在要求的期限前完成全部制作。

我，牛仔伍迪才是真正的英雄！

哇！太逼真了，这都是用电脑制作完成的吗？

不可思议！这才是动画的未来！

看来我当初的直觉是正确的，这部动画真的不错。

哈哈，谢谢您。希望观众也能认可！

飞向宇宙，浩瀚无垠！

哈哈哈！

唉，真希望巴斯光年也能拯救亏损的皮克斯和NeXT……

1995年11月，世界上第一部由电脑设计的3D动画电影《玩具总动员》在美国上映。

嗨，紧张时刻到了，我刚拿到全美第一周的票房统计。

上映第一周，《玩具总动员》的票房2900万美元，稳居排行榜首位！

我郑重宣布，我们的第一部动画电影成功！

耶！

我们的付出终于有收获啦！

导演，这都是你的功劳！

谢谢你给我机会。

《玩具总动员》叫好又叫座，得到观众的一致好评。影片以1.92亿美元的票房刷新了动画电影的纪录，成为1995年美国票房冠军，在全球也缔造了3.6亿美元的票房记录，还为导演约翰·拉塞特赢得了奥斯卡特殊成就奖。

《玩具总动员》上映一星期之后，乔布斯决定将皮克斯公开上市。股票最初定价是每股22美元，但一上市就立刻涨到每股39美元，乔布斯再度成为身价过亿的富豪。

皮克斯声名大噪，成为举世闻名的动画公司。乔布斯9年来的辛苦付出，终于获得了回报。

哈哈，是你们丰富的想象力创造了这一切，今天大家的热情终于感动了世界。

乔布斯，要不是你坚定不移的支持，我们也不会有机会实现梦想。

他的小故事，我的大道理

　　乔布斯经常说："活着就是为了改变世界，难道还有其他什么原因吗？"为了"改变世界"，他要求用极端的方式不断创新。他每天早上都会对着镜子问自己："如果今天是我此生的最后一天，我要干些什么？"这让他每天过得都分外珍惜，让自己的生活不断发生改变。乔布斯留给世界的礼物数不胜数。他的极简主义改变了人们的美学观念，他改变了电脑的使用方式，改变了人们听音乐的方式，改变了电影"造梦"的方式，并使这个世界"提前"进入了移动互联网时代。他为人类留下了一种新的生活方式。乔布斯在每一款苹果产品优雅秀丽的外表下，注入的都是一种挑战既有规则、探索未知领域的创新精神。

　　创新改变世界，乔布斯留给世人最宝贵的财富在于"生命不息、创新不止"。

如果我是他，我会怎么办？

　　乔布斯被董事会赶出了自己亲手创建的公司，他非常痛苦，甚至感到绝望。面临失败和挫折的时候，乔布斯选择了回到原点，从头再来。试想乔布斯从此一蹶不振，我们就看不到《玩具总动员》，更体验不到iPhone手机。如果你是乔布斯，你会怎么办？

如果我是他……

_____

_____

创新改变世界

阅读小脚印

1. 乔布斯为什么重返苹果公司？
2. 每年只拿1美元年薪的乔布斯创造了哪些价值？
3. iMac台式电脑有什么优势？
4. 2005年，乔布斯给斯坦福大学的演讲都讲了什么？

在皮克斯声名大噪、大放异彩的同时，苹果电脑却江河日下，濒临倒闭。

唉！苹果缺乏创新能力，一直在走下坡路，这样下去等不了多久就得关门。

那是我曾经的心血啊，我一手打造的公司……我怎么能看着它慢慢倒下而置之不理呢？

136 用苹果改变世界的IT领袖史蒂夫·乔布斯

苹果终于有救了，我衷心感激您。

1996年，被苹果扫地出门12年后，乔布斯又重返苹果担当顾问。

让我再试一次，就像过去在车库里工作那样，从头再来！

嗯？

在公司遛狗，还在办公室里抽烟！简直让人无法容忍。这是我曾经熟悉的苹果吗？员工的满腔热忱和热火朝天的工作场面到哪里去了？

改变苹果看来得先从改变员工的态度着手，其他的事情可以再等等。

从今天开始，苹果要发生翻天覆地的变化。人员要调整，产品要创新，考核标准要改变，我希望看到不同凡响的苹果。

那些全力以赴工作的人应该得到奖赏，要坚决铲除不劳而获的人，这才是真正的苹果！

此外，我希望大家心中时刻铭记四个字，这才是公司发展的源泉。

创新思考！

Think Different

拥有创新思考的是那些具有独立思想的人；是那些不甘庸庸碌碌、为了追求个人理想而不懈努力的人；是那些想改变世界的人。我希望你们成为这样的人！从今天开始！

耶，我们终于办到了！以这种速度，销量绝对可以超过一百万台！苹果终于重振雄风了！哈哈哈！

乔布斯吸取了以往的教训，根据消费者的需求而不是自己的喜好开发产品。

苹果电脑的新产品持续畅销，苹果员工的工作热情开始高涨起来，对乔布斯也越来越尊重了。此刻，乔布斯作出了新的决定。

我们的iMac已经有两百多万使用者，假如你认为数字惊人，那就回过头想想我们的股票，之前还是每股只值17美元，现在已经飞涨到118美元，苹果市值超过200亿美元。

iPhone创新地引入了多点触控的触摸屏界面，操控更加便捷，再加上App Store上应有尽有的应用软件，成了集照相手机、个人数码助理、媒体播放器以及无线通信设备多项功能于一体的掌上设备，掀起了智能手机热潮，乔布斯再次改变了世界。

与此同时，苹果的平板电脑iPad在推出的第一个月，销量就超过一百万台，并多处断货，出现排队抢购的情况，势头丝毫不比iPhone弱。

苹果如今已经成为世界上最有价值的品牌之一，好多果粉为了参加苹果的新品发布彻夜排队，甚至不惜长途跋涉，只为了抢先买到苹果的最新产品。

2005年，在斯坦福大学的毕业典礼上，乔布斯发表了一场令人动容的演讲。

大概一年以前，我被诊断出癌症。

医生告诉我那很可能是一种无法治愈的胰腺癌，我大概活不过6个月，基本上要准备永别了。

那意味着要把每件事情都安排好，让你的家人尽可能过轻松的生活；那意味着你要说"再见"了。

但是，经过一些检查，我知道我患的是一种可以治的罕见癌症。

那是我最接近死亡的时候，后来医生把我从死亡线上拉了回来，这以后，我更加体会到了生命的弥足珍贵。没有人愿意死，即使人们都想上天堂。

我想告诉大家：你的时间有限，不要浪费时间重复别人的生活。

不要让其他人人喧嚣的观点掩盖你内心真正的声音。我希望你们有勇气去追求自己想要的生活。

"求知若渴，虚心若愚"，我常希望自己能够做到，现在也把这句话送给你们。

在演讲中，乔布斯和毕业生们分享了自己人生中的大起大落、痛苦和挫折，深深地打动了众人，大家从心底里佩服乔布斯面对逆境从头再来的勇气，掌声经久不息。

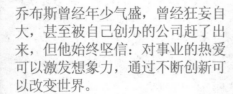

乔布斯曾经年少气盛，曾经狂妄自大，甚至被自己创办的公司赶了出来，但他始终坚信：对事业的热爱可以激发想象力，通过不断创新可以改变世界。

那个曾经充满好奇的小男孩儿，始终保持着创新的激情；那个充满理想与抱负的年轻人，最终震惊了整个世界！如今，乔布斯已经被奉为"神一样的传奇"。

乔布斯一直在与胰腺癌及其他病症作斗争。2010年8月，他辞去苹果公司首席执行官职务。乔布斯任职期间，苹果公司成为美国最具价值的企业。他改变了这个世界，让我们的生活因现代科技充满了更多可能。乔布斯在2011年因病逝世，但他脍炙人口的传奇故事仍在流传。亲爱的小朋友，你有没有可能成为下一个"乔布斯"？

附录

史蒂夫·乔布斯大事记

1955年	诞生于美国加州旧金山，出生一周后，被保罗和克拉拉·乔布斯夫妇收养。
1972年	进入俄勒冈州波特兰的里德学院（Reed College）就读，在第一个学期结束后休学。
1974年	进入雅达利（Atari）公司工作，辞职之后到印度旅行。
1976年	和史蒂夫·沃兹尼亚克（Steve Wozniak）一起成立苹果电脑公司，并推出公司的第一台电脑——Apple Ⅰ。
1977年	Apple Ⅱ问世，掀起一股个人电脑的热潮。
1980年	苹果公司的股票公开上市，25岁的他成为亿万富翁。
1983年	主导开发专家用的电脑——"丽莎"（Lisa），但惨遭滑铁卢。
1984年	推出麦金塔电脑（Macintosh），但销售量不如预期。
1985年	被迫离开苹果公司，成立新的电脑公司NeXT。

1986年	以一千万美元收购皮克斯。
1988年	NeXT开始出售第一台电脑，却没有获得好评。
1995年	皮克斯制作的第一部动画长片《玩具总动员》（Toy Story）票房告捷。
1996年	重回苹果电脑担任顾问。
1997年	成为苹果电脑的临时CEO。
1998年	发布新产品iMac G3，销售量达80万台。
2000年	正式成为苹果电脑的CEO。
2001年	发布MP3随身听iPod。
2007年	发布触摸屏的手机iPhone。
2010年	发布平板电脑iPad。
2011年	因病去世。

我的第一本名人传记漫画书
の
互动园地

亲爱的小朋友们，你们好！

大家都读完了在"我的第一本名人传记漫画书"中介绍的乔布斯的故事了吧？还记得书里面的情节吗？

也许有许多让你印象特别深刻的故事呢！

看完乔布斯的故事之后，适当地休息一下也是很必要的。不知不觉中，你会觉得他就在我们的身边呢！

现在大家拿出铅笔，整理一下脑海中的思绪，先试着回答下面的问题，看看我们有没有把乔布斯的故事都记住吧！

都准备好了吗？那么开始喽~

回忆你记得的小·故事吧~

小朋友们，史蒂夫·乔布斯的哪些故事给你留下了深刻的印象呢？也许你会说都很深刻。

挑出你认为最能感染你的一些故事说说吧！

用苹果改变世界的IT领袖

史蒂夫·乔布斯

我记得的故事

发散思维训练

读过本书，是不是觉得史蒂夫·乔布斯离自己更近了？看到这个名字，你会想到什么？综合思考一下这本书的背景知识和相关内容，一起来发散一下思维吧！

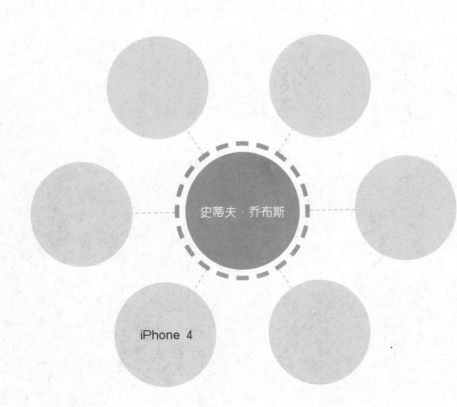

史蒂夫·乔布斯

iPhone 4